ASA Special Series No. 42

Inside the Black Box:

How Arbitral Tribunals Operate and Reach Their Decisions

Bernhard Berger
Michael E. Schneider

Editors

Association Suisse de l'Arbitrage
Schweiz. Vereinigung für Schiedsgerichtsbarkeit
Associazione Svizzera per l'Arbitrato
Swiss Arbitration Association

JURIS

Questions About This Publication

For assistance with shipments, billing or other customer service matters, please call our Customer Services Department at:

1-631-350-2100

To obtain a copy of this book, call our Sales Department:

1-631-351-5430
Fax: 1-631-351-5712

Toll Free Order Line:

1-800-887-4064 (United States and Canada)

See our web page about this book:
www.arbitrationlaw.com

COPYRIGHT 2014
JurisNet, LLC

All rights reserved.

Printed in the United States of America
ISBN 978-1-937518-31-8

JurisNet, LLC
71 New Street
Huntington, New York 11743
USA
www.arbitrationlaw.com

TABLE OF CONTENTS

Foreword	v
About the Editors	vii
About the Moderators and Panelists	ix
Programme of the Conference	1
Welcome Address and Introduction to the Conference Topic .... *Michael E. Schneider*	3
The Legal Framework: Rights and Obligations of Arbitrators in the Deliberations .... *Bernhard Berger*	7
Panel 1: Decision-making and Deliberations: Steps and Issues .... *Moderated by Julian Lew*	13
Organisation of Deliberations .... *Piero Bernardini*	15
Form of Deliberations .... *David W. Rivkin*	21
Drafting the Award .... *Matthias Scherer*	27
Panel 2: Conflict in the Deliberations: Dealing with Bias and Obstruction .... *Moderated by Markus Wirth*	41
Dealing with Bias and Obstruction .... *Phillip Capper*	43
Structuring a Bargaining Process .... *Bernhard F. Meyer*	59
Dealing with Dissenting Opinions .... *Pierre Mayer*	67
Panel 3: Assistance to the Tribunal: Options, Advantages and Dangers .... *Moderated by Michael E. Schneider*	73
Assistance to the Tribunal: an Overview .... *Andrea Meier*	77
Document Production Master and Experts' Facilitator .... *Hans van Houtte*	83
The Secretary to the Arbitral Tribunal .... *Zachary Douglas*	87
The United Nations Compensation Commission's Utilisation of Experts .... *Geoffrey Senogles*	93

Further Written Contributions on the Conference Topic 111

An Essay on the Challenges to Collegiality
.... *William G. Bassler* 111

Six Modest Proposals before You Get to the
Award .... *Nicolas Ulmer* 115

A Short Note on the Decision-making Process
.... *Michael Black* 121

Personal Views on How Arbitral Tribunals
Operate and Reach Their Decisions .... *Nael G. Bunni* 123

Notes and Samples on Tribunal Deliberations
.... *Karl-Heinz Böckstiegel* 129

Arbitration Materials 135

Example of Decision Tree 135

Example of Dissenting Opinion in an Award 144

Example of Dissenting Arbitrator Refusing to
Sign the Award 145

Mandate of Tribunal-Appointed Expert on Scheduling 146

Tribunal Assistant: Scheduling Expert 149

Tribunal Assistant: Scheduling Expert Terms of Reference 151

Tribunal Assistant: Quantification Expert 154

Tribunal Assistant: Quantification Expert Terms of
Reference 155

FOREWORD

This volume of the ASA Special Series reproduces the transcribed presentations and lively discussions at the ASA Annual Full Day Conference of 1 February 2013 held in Zurich on the topic "Inside the Black Box: How Arbitral Tribunals Operate and Reach Their Decisions". Moreover, it serves to publish selected arbitration materials and written contributions we received from a number of distinguished colleagues on the subject of the deliberations and decision-making process, including various forms of assistance to the tribunal.

At the Conference, the first Panel was moderated by Julian Lew and joined by Piero Bernardini, David W. Rivkin and Matthias Scherer as panelists. They provided an overview and interesting insights into the organization of the deliberations, the form of the deliberations and the drafting of the award. A lively debate with the audience ensued in particular on the question as to when the deliberations should commence: After the first round of written submissions? Or immediately after the hearing? Or only later when the post-hearing submissions have been received? This debate demonstrated as a *pars pro toto* that there is and cannot be a "best practice" with regard to the deliberations; it all depends on the circumstances of the case.

The second Panel was composed of Phillip Capper, Bernhard Meyer and Pierre Mayer as panellists and moderated by Markus Wirth. They addressed how to deal with potential conflicts in the deliberations, namely with various forms of bias and obstruction, as well as how to structure what may be called a bargaining process. Somewhat surprisingly, it turned out that, although there are provisions in most arbitration rules to deal with the problems of obstruction and bias, it appears that these are rarely invoked by the other tribunal members in order to resist or defend themselves against inappropriate behaviour of a fellow arbitrator. Are the relevant provisions in the various sets of arbitration rules perhaps wrong or not useful, or should they be revised?

The third Panel brought together Andrea Meier, Hans van Houtte, Zachary Douglas and Geoffrey Senogles as panellists and was moderated by Michael E. Schneider. They provided a detailed overview on various forms of assistance to the arbitral tribunal by third persons (such as tribunal-appointed experts, document production masters, experts' facilitators, secretaries to the tribunal etc.) and addressed the advantages and dangers involved with the utilisation of such assistants. On one hand, it turned out from the presentations and discussions on this topic that the picture of the "lone" arbitrator who does all by himself should be put into perspective. On the other hand, it appears that there has emerged a consensus that more transparency with regard to the use of secretaries and other (legal) assistants would be desirable.

On behalf of ASA Swiss Arbitration Association, we would like to thank the moderators and panellists for all the time and effort they have devoted to the success of the Conference. It was a great pleasure to prepare and navigate through this Conference with such a great number of highly experienced and distinguished arbitrators.

Our special thanks and gratitude go to our Executive Director, Alex McLin, and his Assistant, Loraine de Weck, for the perfect handling of all organisational and administrative matters relating to the Conference, and to Robyn Nott for her impeccable transcription services.

We hope that all those who could make it to Zurich on 1 February 2013 have enjoyed the various contributions and debates as much as we did. Moreover, we hope that this volume of the ASA Special Series provides both interesting and entertaining reading, not only to the participants but also to all those who would have wished to attend.

Berne / Geneva, Summer of 2013
Bernhard Berger
Michael E. Schneider

ABOUT THE EDITORS

Bernhard Berger is a Partner in the international arbitration practice of Kellerhals Attorneys at Law, in Berne, Switzerland. He has served as chair, sole arbitrator, co-arbitrator and counsel in numerous international and domestic arbitrations under the ICC, SCAI, LCIA, SIAC, CAS, and UNCITRAL Rules; and in other ad hoc proceedings. Mr Berger's experience also includes various appearances as legal expert on Swiss arbitration law in arbitration and court proceedings both in Switzerland and abroad; and as counsel in arbitration-related Swiss court proceedings, namely on the recognition and enforcement, setting aside, and revision of awards. Mr Berger has an LL.M. from Harvard Law School and a Ph.D. (Dr. iur.) from the University of Berne Faculty of Law. He has authored numerous treatises and articles in the fields of international arbitration, civil procedure and contract law, including *International and Domestic Arbitration in Switzerland* (2010) and *Allgemeines Schuldrecht* (2012).

Michael E. Schneider is the President of the Swiss Arbitration Association (ASA). Mr Schneider, founding Partner of LALIVE in Geneva, has practiced international arbitration for more than 35 years, acting as counsel before arbitration tribunals under various rules, including those of the ICC, ICSID, LCIA, Stockholm Institute, the Cairo Regional Centre for International Commercial Arbitration (CRCICA), European Development Fund, UNCITRAL and before other international bodies, including the WTO Appellate Body and the United Nations Compensation Commission (UNCC). He has also been sitting as arbitrator (chair, sole or co-arbitrator) under the rules of many institutions in Switzerland and abroad. Mr Schneider is Vice Chair of the ICC Commission on Arbitration, and has been a member of several of its working groups (1998 Revision of the ICC Rules, Construction, Pre-arbitral Referee). He chaired the UNCITRAL Working Group II (Arbitration) on the revision of the Arbitration Rules (2006 to 2010) and is a member of the executive committee of the Dubai International Arbitration Centre (DIAC) and of its Board of Trustees as well as a member of the Board of Trustees of the Cairo Regional Center of International Commercial Arbitration (CRCICA).

ABOUT THE MODERATORS AND PANELISTS

Piero Bernardini is an Of Counsel in the law firm Ughi e Nunziante in Rome. He was General Counsel of Eni Group (1980-1985) and served on the Board of Eni and as an Executive Committee member (1986-1990) as well as Chair of international arbitration—LUISS University—Rome (1982-2005). He is the President of the Italian Arbitration Association, a Member of the ICCA Council and has served as Vice-President of the ICC International Court of Arbitration (2000-2006). Further, he is a Member of the ICSID panel of conciliators and arbitrators by the Italian Government Appointment. Mr Bernardini has been acting as arbitrator, president of arbitral tribunals, member of ICSID annulment committees and counsel in more than 300 commercial and investment treaty cases, under the rules of ICSID, ICC, LCIA, NAI, Cairo Centre, UNCITRAL, CAM, AIA, VIAC, and SCC. He is a frequent speaker, moderator or chairman in national and international congresses and seminars and an author of numerous books and articles dealing with problems regarding petroleum, state contracts, investment protection, commercial contracts, and arbitration.

Phillip Capper is Partner and Head of International Arbitration at White & Case in London. He has been involved in countless international disputes as arbitrator, advocate, mediator, legal assessor, or adviser. As arbitrator, Phillip has chaired ICC, LCIA and UNCITRAL arbitral tribunals, and has served as sole arbitrator and party-appointed arbitrator in ICC and LCIA arbitrations. Phillip is a highly regarded advocate in arbitration. As counsel, he has acted under the rules of ICC, LCIA, and the Stockholm, Madrid and Prague Chambers of Commerce, as well as in contractual mediations and ad-hoc arbitrations under UNCITRAL Rules and otherwise. For the ICC in Paris he led small working groups drafting model clauses for ICC arbitration and ADR, and for use with the ICC Rules for Expertise. Formerly Chairman of the Faculty of Law at Oxford University, he is also now Nash Professor of Engineering Law at King's College London, teaching International Arbitration and Construction Law and directs the annual International Diploma Course for the Chartered Institute of Arbitrators in Oxford. Phillip is an Honorary Member of the Society of Construction Law, Honorary Member of the Royal Institution of Chartered Surveyors, and Honorary President of the Adjudication Society.

Zachary Douglas is a Barrister at Matrix Chambers and Professor of International Law at the Graduate Institute in Geneva. He has acted as counsel in numerous investment treaty arbitrations and commercial arbitrations under the ICC, LCIA, SCC, UNCITRAL and ICSID Arbitration Rules and in cases before the English courts and other common law courts relating to state immunity, human rights, humanitarian law, state responsibility, state succession, challenges to investment treaty awards and money-laundering. He has been appointed as an arbitrator in more than forty investment treaty and commercial arbitrations, including as chairman and as sole arbitrator in half of those. Zachary is fluent in both Russian and French and has conducted bilingual arbitration proceedings in both languages. He has been instructed by States in proceedings before the International Court of Justice and the European Court of Human Rights and has also been counsel in dozens of cases before the Court of Arbitration for Sport, having formerly represented the International Olympic Committee. Zachary is the author of *The International Law of Investment Claims* (Cambridge University Press, 2009), which is one of the leading texts on the subject as well as numerous articles on public and private international law and international arbitration. He has a PhD from Cambridge University. Zachary has been ranked in the first tier of barristers for public international law and international arbitration for several years by *Chambers London* and *Chambers Global*.

Hans van Houtte, LL.M. Harvard, is President of the Iran-United States Claims Tribunal (The Hague) and teaches arbitration at the University of Leuven (Belgium), where he held successively the chair of international public law and international private law, while also teaching international business law. He has been a member of the Brussels Bar since 1971 and withdrew as litigation and arbitration Partner at Stibbe (Brussels) in 2000. Since then he has been an independent arbitrator. He sits frequently as an arbitrator in commercial and investment disputes (ICC, LCIA, ICSID, NAFTA, UNCITRAL, ICDR, CEP ANI, DIS, Vienna Centre, DIAC, SCAI, etc.) and has rendered over 200 awards. He also sat as a Commissioner for Real Property in Bosnia, was a member of the United Nations Compensation Commission (UNCC), an arbitrator at the Dormant Bank Accounts Tribunal (CRT, Zurich) and was President of the Eritrea-Ethiopia Claims Commission. He was also vice-president of CEPANI. He can be reached at hans.vanhoutte@law.kuleuven.be.

ABOUT THE MODERATORS AND PANELISTS

Julian Lew has been involved with International Arbitration for well over 30 years as both as a practitioner and academic. He has acted as counsel and advised parties in all kinds of international arbitrations. He is now a full-time Arbitrator and sits as chairman of arbitral tribunals, sole arbitrator and co-arbitrator under all the major international arbitration systems, including ICC, ICSID, LCIA, SCC, SIAC, UNCITRAL, and Swiss Rules. Until 2005, he was a Partner at Herbert Smith, and head of its International Arbitration Practice. He is Professor of Law and Head of the School of International Arbitration, Queen Mary, University of London. He has written and published numerous books and articles on international arbitration including *Applicable Law on International Arbitration* (1978) and *Comparative International Commercial Arbitration* (2003) (with Mistelis and Kröll). He also has lectured extensively in many countries around the world on all aspects of International Arbitration. He is a member of the ICC International Court of Arbitration (UK) and a member of the Council of the ICC Institute of World Business Law. He was the Chairman of the ICC Commission Task Force on Intellectual Property and International Arbitration, and is currently joint chairman of the ICC Commission Task Force on Costs in International Arbitration. He has an LLB from the University of London and a Doctorate in private international law from the Catholic University of Louvain.

Pierre Mayer is one of the world's leading authorities in international dispute resolution. He has concentrated his practice in arbitration for more than 25 years, both as Counsel and as Arbitrator in international trade, joint ventures and industrial cooperation, technology transfer, and oil & gas distribution under the rules of ICSID, ICC and UNCITRAL. Mr Mayer is listed in *The Legal 500 Paris*, *Chambers*, *Practical Law Company's Which Lawyer?*, and *Décideurs Stratégie Finance Droit* as one of the world's most respected legal scholars, particularly for his expertise in private international law, a subject he has taught as a Professor of law since 1984 at Sorbonne University in Paris. Before joining Dechert LLP as a Partner in 2006, Mr Mayer was Counsel at Coudert Brothers in Paris for nearly 20 years and then at Clifford Chance as counsel, chairman or co-arbitrator, Mr Mayer has lent his expertise to a long list of arbitration cases in various industrial sectors and countries. His other professional activities include: President of French Committee on International Private Law, Associate member of the *Institut de Droit International*, Member of Council of the ICC Institute of World Business Law, former President of the Committee on

International Commercial Arbitration of the International Law Association, former President of the Committee on Private International Law of the *Union Internationale des Avocats* (UIA). Mr Mayer has authored numerous publications in the fields of international arbitration, international private and commercial law.

Andrea Meier is a Partner in the international arbitration practice of Wartmann & Merker in Zurich, Switzerland. She represents clients before international arbitral tribunals and state courts in commercial matters, including disputes arising from industrial and infrastructure projects, banking and finance, and M&A transactions. She has also served as sole arbitrator, co-arbitrator and secretary in numerous international and domestic arbitrations under the ICC, SCAI, ICDR, and UNCITRAL Rules, and in other ad hoc proceedings. Ms Meier is co-chair of ASA below 40, the young practitioners' group of the Swiss Arbitration Association. She has an LL.M. from Harvard Law School and a Ph.D. (Dr. iur.) from the University of Zurich Faculty of Law. Ms Meier has authored various articles in the fields of international arbitration and civil procedure, including a chapter on the Emergency Arbitrator in the 2nd edition of the Zuberbühler/Müller/Habegger *Swiss Rules Commentary* and several chapters, including one on multi-party arbitration, in *Arbitration in Switzerland: The Practitioner's Guide* by M. Arroyo.

Bernhard F. Meyer is a Senior Arbitrator and Arbitration Counsel at MME Partners, Zurich, Switzerland. He was involved in more than 200 international arbitrations as chairman, arbitrator and counsel under the Rules of the ICC, SWISS CHAMBERS, AAA/ICDR, LCIA, HKIAC, SIAC, VIENNA RULES, WIPO, UNCITRAL and others. He is Vice-Chair of ASA, Chairman of the ICC Commission on Arbitration in Switzerland, Jurisdictional Council Member of the Inter-Pacific Bar Association (IPBA), Member of the ABA Arbitration Commission and he is holding other functions in various arbitration bodies. Mr Meyer studied law at the University of Zurich (Dr. iur.) and Northwestern University School of Law, Chicago, Illinois, USA (LL.M). He is a Fellow of the Chartered Institute of Arbitrators (FCIArb), a Fellow of the Singapore Institute of Arbitrators (SCIArb), and has authored or co-authored a significant number of publications in the arbitration field as well as in other fields of international commercial law.

David W. Rivkin is a Litigation Partner of Debevoise & Plimpton LLP in the firm's New York and London offices, has broad experience in the areas of international litigation and arbitration. He has handled international arbitrations throughout the world and before virtually every major arbitration institution. Subjects of these arbitrations have included long-term energy concessions, investment treaties, joint venture agreements, insurance coverage, construction contracts, distribution agreements and intellectual property, among others. Mr Rivkin also represents companies in transnational litigation in the US, including the enforcement of arbitral awards and arbitration agreements. He is consistently ranked as one of the top international dispute resolution practitioners in the world and has been consistently ranked among the top ten international arbitration practitioners worldwide in *Chambers Global* which has called him "among the very, very best", has noted that he is "wonderful as counsel and wonderful as arbitrator" and is well regarded for producing "high-quality work that is fair and balanced." In 2012, the American Lawyer's Am Law Litigation Daily named Mr Rivkin one of two "Global Lawyers of the Year." In 2011, the National Law Journal named him one of the country's "Most Influential Attorneys". He has also been ranked as the leading American in international arbitration in *Who's Who Legal* (2013) and in Euromoney's *Expert Guide to the Leading Lawyers: Best of the Best* (2013). Mr Rivkin has served on the boards of many arbitration institutions, and he is currently also the Vice President of the International Bar Association.

Matthias Scherer is a Partner of LALIVE (Geneva/Zurich). He has practiced international arbitration for 20 years, acting as counsel before arbitration tribunals under various rules, including those of ICC, UNCITRAL, ICSID, Swiss Chambers, LCIA, and CAS. He is regularly appointed as arbitrator by leading institutions, such as ICC, Swiss Chambers, ICSID, Stockholm Chamber of Commerce, DIAC, LCIA, and PCA in Switzerland and abroad. He frequently represents parties in arbitral matters before the Swiss Supreme Court. Matthias Scherer is a past vice-chair of the International Bar Association's arbitration committee and of the arbitration committee of the Swiss Chambers of Commerce. Matthias Scherer is the editor of the journal of the Swiss Arbitration Association, the ASA Bulletin, co-editor of the Swiss International Arbitration Law Reports, and a member of the Board of Editors of the International Arbitration Law Review (London).

Geoffrey Senogles is a chartered accountant Vice President, Forensic Accounting in Charles River Associates in Geneva and London. His core practice is acting as expert witness on financial damages matters in international arbitration—treaty and commercial. He has testified in arbitrations under ICSID, UNCITRAL and ICC rules and involving claims across a diverse range of sectors. Particular sector experience includes; power, energy, telecommunications and commodity trading. He also leads business valuation, financial investigation and oversight mandates. Assignments have taken him extensively to the Middle East as well as Africa and North America. Between 2000 and 2003, he worked on staff at the United Nations Compensation Commission. He has testified to the Iran-US Claims Tribunal and has spoken at legal conferences, seminars. He lectures on financial damages on the 'MIDS' LL.M. programme at the University of Geneva and is listed in the 2012 and 2013 Who's Who in Commercial Arbitration.

Markus Wirth is a Senior Partner in the Litigation / Arbitration Team of HOMBURGER in Zurich. He has more than 35 years' practice in contract and corporate law, advising on transactions and as counsel in commercial and civil law disputes. As arbitration counsel, Markus Wirth has represented Swiss and foreign companies as well as foreign governments and state organizations in numerous arbitrations seated in Switzerland and abroad under a variety of institutional rules and ad hoc proceedings. Today he acts mainly as arbitrator in which capacity he has by now served in over 130 international arbitrations in Switzerland and abroad (Europe, North America and Asia), in the majority as chairman of the panel or as sole arbitrator. He is the immediate past president, and honorary president, of the Swiss Arbitration Association (ASA), a member of the ICC International Court of Arbitration and a Fellow of the Chartered Institute of Arbitrators, London. He presently chairs ASA's task force on the revision of Chapter 12 of the Swiss International Private Law Act on international arbitration in Switzerland.

Programme of the Conference

1. **Welcome Address and Introduction to the Conference Topic**

   Michael E. Schneider, President of ASA, Lalive, Geneva

2. **The Legal Framework: Rights and Obligations of Arbitrators in the Deliberations**

   Bernhard Berger, Kellerhals, Berne

3. **Panel 1: Decision-making and Deliberations: Steps and Issues**

   How should deliberations as a rule be organised? At what time should opinions be formed and expressed? Who goes first? Are there "best practices"? Is there a difference according to the type of decision (partial/final; procedural/merits)? Unanimous and majority decisions; decisions by the chairperson alone. Drafting the decision: when? by whom? The chairperson? The arbitrator with the best drafting and linguistic skills, allocation of tasks?

   Moderator: *Julian D.M. Lew QC*, 20 Essex Street, London

   Panelists: *Piero Bernardini*, Ughi e Nunziante, Rome

   　　　　　　David W. Rivkin, Debevoise & Plimpton, London

   　　　　　　Matthias Scherer, Lalive, Geneva

4. **Panel 2: Conflict in the Deliberations: Dealing with Bias and Obstruction**

   How to deal with bias and obstruction? Reporting obstructive behaviour and misconduct by arbitrators, is it possible? Desirable? Dissenting opinions: should they be avoided? How to deal with them? Should the decision on costs be used as a "sweetener"? How to deal with stalemate (no majority found)?

   Moderator: *Markus Wirth*, Homburger, Zurich

   Panellists: *Phillip Capper*, White & Case, London

   　　　　　　Bernhard Meyer, MME Partners, Zurich

   　　　　　　Pierre Mayer, Dechert, Paris

5. **Panel 3: Assistance to the Tribunal: Options, Advantages and Dangers**

   Forms of assistance to the Tribunal: administrative and organisational; document management; drafting and editing; technical understanding; legal research. Advisors to the Tribunal: are they permissible and useful? Under what conditions? How to preserve the integrity of the process and the responsibility of the tribunal for the award?

   Moderator: *Michael E. Schneider*, President of ASA, Lalive, Geneva

   Panellists: *Andrea Meier*, Wartmann & Merker, Zurich

   Hans van Houtte, President of the Iran-US Claims Tribunal

   Zachary Douglas, Matrix Chambers, London

   Geoffrey Senogles, Charles River Associates, Geneva

Welcome Address and Introduction to the Conference Topic

Michael E. Schneider

MICHAEL E. SCHNEIDER:

Good morning, Ladies and Gentlemen, ASA members and friends!

I can see the conference about deliberations has started with very active deliberations among you so it is difficult to get you all sitting down so that we can start with our conference. I can see the ten minutes for my opening speech are already over!

I would like to start with a few words from inside the Association and the first subject I will touch on is very sad news. Daniel Wehrli, our Vice-President and for many years a member of our board, has left us. He was a highly respected lawyer and arbitrator and made important contributions to the work of the Association and arbitration in general. I mention merely his contribution to the elaboration of the Swiss Rules and also his work in UNCITRAL where he represented ASA. Those who have worked with him and who knew him well appreciated his conscientiousness and his balanced judgment. His death was a tragedy for all of us and also a warning to us. May I ask you to stand up for a moment in thoughts to him.

[Short pause]

As to forward looking news of our Association, there are a number of recent developments. Many of you who were at our last conference have met already Alex McLin our Executive Director, and since then we have an assistant, Loraine de Weck. There she is at the back: the smiling face of ASA! She is based in Geneva and in Zurich. We have now two offices where you are welcome to visit our work. Alex and Loraine are in these offices and they are shifting to keep the balance between our centres.

To succeed Daniel we have now Bernhard Meyer who stepped in as an interim Vice-President. He will join Elliot Geisinger as the second Vice-President in the Bureau of the Association.

There will be great changes in the Articles of Association. All of you have received a draft. We got some feedback from the members about the draft Articles of Association and the Board yesterday sat and polished them. You will receive them in the next few weeks and will then have an opportunity to vote electronically — another first in our

Association—about these Articles of Association. Then in the next conference on 4 October 2013 we will also have the General Assembly Meeting and we will then vote for the first time on the new structures, the new President and the new Board provided by these Statutes.

Note down the general meeting is 4 October. The conference is another very interesting and not very much discussed subject, confidentiality, but not confidentiality about arbitration but in arbitration, all the issues that arise when you have confidentiality. Elliot Geisinger is preparing this conference which will be a very interesting one on 4 October.

We are preparing for next January the next round of the ASA prize on advocacy. You have on our website the form for suggestions so please look at it and send us your suggestions.

The last word is thanks to our sponsors who invited us yesterday to the reception. You had their names before you when you walked in. Thanks for your support.

For the conference today it is an unusual subject, or it was until ASA picked it up. We announced our conference two years ago and now you have the IBA in Bogota who is talking about the same subject. You have other studies: Edna Sussman has an inquiry about how arbitrators go about; Sophie Nappert had a similar project. You also find some aspects on our conference in the conference binder.

The objective of this conference is not, as David Lawson experienced recently, a cookbook how you deliberate and how you write your award; the objective is to give an overview on the variety of situations and the diversity of the manner in which you can deal with it. One of the main aspects is that we feel and hear how different situations can be addressed differently. We have the thoughts and experiences of our distinguished speakers. You have their CVs in the conference binder.

We have made an inquiry in the ASA Bulletin and through many letters inviting arbitrators to let us know their experiences and let us have materials from their practice. I have to say the number of feedback was surprisingly low. It may have been that these distinguished and busy arbitrators had other things to do; partly it may be due to the sensitivity of the subject. There are things you do not want to talk about. In fact, recently I heard a distinguished experienced arbitrator talk about arguing in the Tribunal and I said "Very interesting, can you make a note for our file so that you share this experience?" He sat down and wrote and interesting note, circulated it among his own arbitration group and they said "No, you cannot publish that." That is part of the difficulty of having this sort of information at this conference. We will look at our speakers, our panellists and we will look to you. We have a large section in our programme for your contributions and we hope that the exchange we will have will be enriching for all of us.

One thing that is important is that the discussion will be recorded. It is therefore important that you wait until you have the microphone before you speak so that everything you say will be in our book which we will publish after the conference with the materials in the conference folder, with the presentations at the conference and with what you have contributed to the subject.

The project has been prepared primarily by Bernhard Berger who had a big task. You all know Bernhard Berger from Berger & Kellerhals, who is a guide for us through many difficulties and the interesting things of arbitration in Switzerland. He had a great job in setting up the programme and the contacts with the speakers making sure that they are all here, making sure that they know what they have to say and making sure they are well prepared which, as you will see, they all are. He was assisted by Alex and Loraine for the preparation.

Bernhard will be opening the conference as you see in the programme. We will start with an overview of the legal problems that arise before we engage into the more practice-orientated programme where we have three main subjects: the first one is the decision making process itself, how do Arbitrators go about making decisions, how do they organise the process, when and how they go about it. The second panel deals with obstruction, dissent, and how that can be handled, a subject of great importance. There have been colleagues of ours who said that because of obstruction and dissent you should forget about the party-appointed arbitrators, but a much more constructive approach which is more in line with what we are used to doing in arbitration is to see how you face the problems that arise from some of the party-appointed arbitrators. The last topic is about assistance: what assistance can arbitrators receive and how that should be dealt with. Now we start with Bernhard Berger.

The Legal Framework: Rights and Obligations of Arbitrators in the Deliberations

Bernhard Berger

BERNHARD BERGER:

Good morning ladies and gentlemen, a warm welcome also from my side to this conference and many thanks to Michael for your very kind introduction.

Before turning to the substance of my short presentation please note that at tab 5 of the conference binder you will find a more detailed written report on my speech.

I was instructed, I have to say, by Michael to set the floor by outlining the rights and obligations of arbitrators in the deliberations. But let me first briefly reflect why we are talking about the deliberations as a black box. What is a black box? If you do not have an idea or do not know, you obviously "Google". That is what I did and Wikipedia has told me that a black box is a device whose inner workings are unknown, more precisely a device that can be seen only from the outside.

What does that mean? You see the input, the output and the transfer characteristics but not the internal workings. In terms of arbitration, we could say, and this obviously from the parties' perspective, you know the arguments and motions put forward in the proceedings, that is the input; you can see the result in the form of the dispositive section of the award, that is the output; and you can try to understand the reasons given for the decision in the award, that will be the transfer element. All the rest that may have happened in the deliberations remains undisclosed and undiscovered: for example, is there a relatively mild decision on the quantum of damages as a bargaining chip for the unanimous affirmation of liability?

What causes this black box? To me I think the answer is simple: because the parties are not allowed to attend the deliberations let alone to participate in them. The confidentiality of the deliberations is seen as an inherent feature of arbitration.

Determining the process and timing:

In my view determining the process and timing of the deliberations is an obligation but also a right of the arbitrators. Arbitration laws and rules are—interestingly enough—mostly silent on this matter. Even the 1996 UNCITRAL Notes on Organising Arbitral Proceedings do not address the deliberations either. Setting the framework for the deliberations therefore largely remains a matter for the discretion of the arbitrators.

One of the driving factors in this regard may be whether the award has to be made by a unanimous vote, by a majority or even, if there is no majority, by the presiding arbitrator alone. We will hear more about these problems from Panel 1 and Panel 2 later today.

Participation in the deliberations:

Participation in the deliberations is certainly also both a right and an obligation of each of the arbitrators, as accurately emphasised by the relatively new Article 382(1) of the Swiss Code of Civil Procedure. It may therefore be claimed that the process of deliberations was faulty if, for instance, two arbitrators have prevented their fellow from effectively participating in the process, like this has been (albeit unsuccessfully) claimed in the well-known CME case.

On the other hand, when an arbitrator, and usually a party-appointed one, refuses to participate in the deliberations without valid reasons, the remaining members of the panel should be authorised to proceed with the making of the award. The latter principle is well illustrated by Article 382(2) of the Swiss Code of Civil Procedure. It states that in such a case the majority may deliberate and decide in the absence of such arbitrator.

However, the right to participate also has limits, as shown by, I would think, a most accurate statement of a Swedish Court of Appeal in the already mentioned CME case. In that decision the Court held that where the award shall be made by majority, a minority arbitrator cannot prolong the deliberations by demanding continued discussions in an attempt to persuade the others as to the correctness of his opinion.

Duties of care, diligence and expedition:

The duties of care and diligence of an arbitrator obviously includes devoting the necessary time and attention to the issues at stake and analysing the submissions and evidence with the necessary skills and ability. Furthermore, the arbitrators are expected to conduct the arbitration, as we all know, and in particular also in the deliberations, with expedition.

What remedies are available if the arbitrators, or some of them, fail to comply with these duties? The last resort obviously is to have such arbitrator or arbitrators replaced. However, as far as I am aware, this remedy is very rarely used and the question is: why is that? The replacement of an arbitrator is a rather time-consuming and burdensome process and therefore often not in the best interests of the case. It is therefore often more convenient for the other arbitrators simply to drag along a defaulting arbitrator than going through the process of replacement.

Impartiality and independence:

The principle of impartiality and independence is common ground but it is important to note that a lack of impartiality often transpires only towards the end of the proceedings, in particular during the deliberations.

There are arbitrators for whom, for whatever reasons, it is unthinkable to accept a decision against the party that has designated them. In such occasion it is important that the presiding arbitrator properly records each step of the proceedings that take place in the deliberations and decision-making process in his internal file. This may prove to be very helpful in case of a subsequent challenge against the award on the grounds of any alleged irregularity in the deliberations and in the decision-making process, as that has also been unsuccessfully claimed in the already mentioned CME case.

Application of the law:

This duty one may think is a matter of course, but it must be highlighted as this obligation particularly unfolds in the course of the deliberations. This is so because in many, if not in most, jurisdictions as we all know there is no meaningful remedy against a failure of the tribunal to apply the law or against a wrongful application of the law.

Therefore, there may be a certain temptation perhaps to think in certain occasions that arbitration is some kind of free ticket to decide whatever the panel may consider as being just and appropriate without having regard too much to the law. However, I think that any misuse of this kind is a serious threat and seriously compromises arbitration as a whole. It is, therefore, not surprising that voices have increased in the more recent past who suggest that the self-restraint of the courts in this regard should be reconsidered.

Obligation to fulfil the mission *in personam*:

As a matter of principle, the arbitrator's mission as a mandate implies that we all have to perform the duties of an arbitrator in person; after all we have been selected to perform this function because of our own skills, qualifications, experience, reputation, and so forth. It would, therefore, obviously not be permissible to delegate the duty to participate in the deliberations and voting to a third party, let alone to another arbitrator, for example to the chairperson.

This prohibition shines through, as I would assume, accurately in Rule 15.2 of the ICSID Arbitration Rules in that it states, on one hand, that the members of the Tribunal shall take part in the deliberations and, on the other hand, emphasises that no other persons should be admitted to this process.

What remedies could be invoked in case of a wrongful delegation? In my view a violation of this obligation would give rise to an annulment or non-recognition of an award on the grounds of an irregular composition of the Tribunal.

Assistance to the tribunal:

The prohibition of delegation seems to disregard to a certain extent that arbitrators quite frequently seek assistance in the course of the proceedings from various sources. Perhaps the best known of all these examples is the famous secretary to the tribunal. One of the major questions is whether these assistants to the tribunal may attend the deliberations. In my view the best answer may again be taken from Rule 15.2 of the ICSID Rules: the tribunal may consult with the parties before allowing third parties to attend but the tribunal should have the final word on this. Panel 3 will address these issues in more detail.

Duty of confidentiality:

Confidentiality of the deliberation means, on one hand, that the deliberations take place in a closed session, in particular that there is no entry for the parties. On the other hand, confidentiality means that each arbitrator has an obligation and is bound to keep the deliberations and the result of voting confidential both from the parties and from any third parties. In my view, Article 9 of the IBA Rules of Ethics for International Arbitrators still provides an accurate description of the scope and limits of the confidentiality of the deliberations: an arbitrator shall not provide the parties with any information on the course of the deliberations and votes unless exceptional circumstances so compel.

An interesting question, in my view, is to determine who may invoke the right to the confidentiality of the deliberations. If you analyse various books you will see that some say it is the parties, whereas it appears that the majority seem to support the view that the confidentiality of the deliberations and votes serves to protect the arbitrators.

But from what do the arbitrators have to be protected? We should not lose sight of the fact that State Court judges apparently do not need such protection. Their deliberations in civil and commercial matters frequently take place in the open or in public, at least in Switzerland.

I therefore think the answer is a more pragmatic one. In my view, the main purpose of the confidentiality of the deliberations in international arbitration is simply to ensure that the parties do not find out or hear about the result of the award before its notification.

Why is that important? Because it sometimes takes a long time between the date on which the panel formally takes the decision and closes the deliberations and the date on which the final product, in the form of the award, can be notified to the parties. If we imagine that a party during that time already knew that it is going to win or lose the case, it may be tempted to take unfair advantage of this information. For example, it may be tempted to commence taking adverse measures, like for instance filing unjustified challenges against the arbitrators or divesting assets in order to prevent future enforcement and so forth.

What remedies can be invoked in case of an unlawful disclosure? A breach of confidentiality may give rise to a claim for damages against the arbitrator who fails to comply with it. But we all know that it is normally a very hard case to substantiate any such damage. On the other hand, I think it is difficult to imagine that the award as such may be affected by an unlawful disclosure of confidential information stemming from the deliberations.

Dissenting opinions:

Coming from the principle of confidentiality of the deliberations it is difficult to understand the concept of published dissenting opinions. But, despite this, dissenting opinions seem to have become accepted instruments in international arbitration. Whether we should have more of them is another question.

Some authors consider that there is a fundamental right to disclose dissenting opinions under any circumstances. I personally do not believe that this is an acceptable approach. The Swiss Federal Supreme Court held that, unless the parties have expressly excluded the notification of a dissenting opinion, it is a matter for the Tribunal or the majority of its members to decide whether, and in what form, a dissent should be made available to the parties. In my view, this is the sensible approach.

Therefore, only in exceptional circumstances should a minority arbitrator be allowed to produce a dissent to the parties without the consent of the majority. Such a situation may exist as stated, for example, in the already mentioned Article 9 of the IBA Rules of Ethics when the dissenting arbitrator—and I would add acting in good faith—considers it his duty to disclose "any material misconduct or fraud on the part of his fellow arbitrators."

Again, here the question arises: are there any remedies in case an arbitrator unduly publishes his dissenting opinion? In most cases I do not think so. What remains, however, in my view, is a serious breach of the principle of collegiality vis-a-vis the other arbitrators. We will hear more about this subject from Panel 2 later today.

That brings me to the end of this short overview. I say let us open the black box and look inside. The floor now belongs to Panel 1 which is chaired by Julian Lew.

Panel 1

Decision-making and Deliberations: Steps and Issues

Moderated by Julian Lew

JULIAN LEW:

Good morning, ladies and gentlemen. First of all, thank you to Michael E. Schneider and Bernhard Berger for their introductions this morning and a personal thank you to them and ASA for this invitation to me to moderate this first session today.

This ASA conference, which I have only managed to attend on several occasions, is a major event in the international arbitration world and well known for the content that it has and the extent of views that are expressed. I hope we will be able to benefit from that during this opening session. There is no monopoly or exclusivity on knowledge and experience and these opportunities to share ideas and experiences are extremely valuable.

Our topic this morning is how decisions are made in arbitration and when should decisions be made in arbitrations. This involves both theory, when one sits here cold and says this is the way we think it ought to be — and of course a great deal comes from theory in the way one approaches things — and, on the other hand, there are practical issues, and every case differs on its facts, on the circumstances and in particular the composition of the tribunal and the personalities that are there.

A big question is who takes control? Is it the two party-nominated or co-arbitrators or is it the chairman? Many of you will have some experience, or at least know, of the system that was prevalent in England for many years where the party-appointed arbitrators would only bring in the third arbitrator if they could not agree. We had this concept of the umpire who was the third person. In some industries they bring the third arbitrator in from the beginning so they do not have to repeat everything. The whole question would then arise does he sit there and say nothing and express no views or should he participate? That is largely history but it does bring through the issue of how deliberations should be conducted and who should take the driving role in that. We will hear more about that today. There is probably no correct answer on timing and procedure. We will hear war stories, which lawyers greatly enjoy sharing with others, of the way these hearings take place.

We will try and put some light into the black box that Bernhard Berger so clearly talked about. He described the secrecy and confidentiality of deliberations and the absence of rules and of course the crossroads that one experiences in international cases with different legal mentalities, cultures and approaches. We will hopefully talk a fair amount about this in this session.

We are privileged to have three very experienced and well-known individuals to make our presentations today. We will hear first from three of them. I am delighted to introduce Matthias Scherer on my left, David W. Rivkin on my right, and Piero Bernardini to my further right. None of them need an introduction, certainly in this audience who know the international arbitration world. Their full CVs are here in the conference materials. If I try to sum up, the one distinction they have is that Piero Bernardini comes from Italy, David W. Rivkin comes from the United States and Matthias Scherer is from Switzerland. In reality in our industry as arbitrators they are all internationalists and whilst they might come from different backgrounds, over the years that international approach, which is the key to the arbitration industry, has been honed which brings the centrality.

When we talk about deliberations it reminds me of a case that I am just finishing at the present time where I have one arbitrator from Sweden, another from Russia and I am chairing that case. I will not say any more other than when we shared our views the decision was unanimous, the answer had no differences but there were different ways of thinking to get to that result. None was right, but we came to the same conclusion. That is the key of our speakers this morning.

I am going to turn to our three speakers. Piero Bernardini will go first, then David W. Rivkin, then Matthias Scherer and then I will open the discussion to the floor. We will invite your comments and discussions and we will come back to talk a little bit more about that after our speakers.

Organisation of Deliberations

Piero Bernardini

PIERO BERNARDINI:

Thank you Julian and thank you to ASA and Michael E. Schneider for inviting me to speak before this distinguished audience.

The first point I will have to deal with is identifying the issues to be decided. As we all know, the award is commonly defined as a decision by an arbitral tribunal which disposes in a final way, in all or in part, the issues submitted by the parties for decision. The first task in the deliberation process for the tribunal is to identify what issues are we supposed to decide to make an award.

Those issues are normally extracted, if I may say so, by the tribunal from the parties' pleadings and especially the relief sought. This is not always so easy a task because the parties sometimes have not well defined their positions so it will be up to the tribunal to ask the parties to submit a kind of final conclusion in which the issues they wish to be decided by the tribunal are clearly spelt out.

Why are issues to be decided by an award so important: because the arbitrator, as the international judge, is bound by the *petita partium*. If an arbitral tribunal decides *infra petita*, as we know, the award may be subject to annulment by the competent court or, in case for example of application of the English Arbitration Act, may be subject to the reconsideration by the arbitral tribunal by order of the court.

The first distinction I believe to be made is between questions of procedure and substantive questions. Questions of procedure are normally decided by an order. Questions of substance, the issue which I have been talking until now, have to be decided by an award. There are different rules governing decision and deliberation, a question of procedure with respect to a question of substance: the first to be decided by an order, the latter by an award.

The tribunal may delegate the decision or questions of procedure to the chairman—as Bernhard Berger mentioned this before—or, as under the Italian Code of Civil Procedure, the acquisition of means of evidence may be delegated by the tribunal to one member of the tribunal.

Normally questions of procedure are decided by unanimous vote of the tribunal. In my experience I have never seen a majority to be formed on a question of procedure, but there may be cases of some difficult problems to be solved, like interim measures of protection or decisions on requests for production of documents, in which the deliberation might be more complex than expected.

What is important is identifying what are the questions to be decided by an order as being of a procedural nature or rather by an award as being rather questions of substance. There is a famous well-known French case, Braspetro, in which the decision taken by the tribunal by way of an order on the assumption that it was a procedural matter was annulled by the Court of Appeal in Paris in 1999 because in examining the nature and the fact of that decision the court determined that it was rather a matter for an award than for an order.

Contrary to deliberation for questions of procedure, the deliberation for substantive issues follows more formal rules. They have to be taken in private, as we heard from Bernhard Berger, and this means to the exclusion of any third party, including the secretary of the tribunal, except if the tribunal decides otherwise.

The practical effect of this confidentiality requirement may be indicated by the experience I had in one situation in which I sat as arbitrator with an English judge as chairman. During the deliberation process the fellow arbitrator came to the deliberation accompanied by his secretary. Then he had to abide by the order of the president that the personal secretary of the arbitrator could not attend the deliberation because the deliberation was secret and confidential. At the end, the result was that since that arbitrator knew almost nothing about the case while his secretary was fully informed he had to keep silent during the deliberation process and we reached a majority quite easily without any participation by that arbitrator, which to me is a poor service to arbitration in general and a breach of the duty owed by any arbitrator to the parties.

The process of deliberation is the moment of truth regarding the actual independence and impartiality required from party-appointed arbitrators beyond what they have stated initially in their declaration of independence or notified subsequently during the course of the proceedings. It is only at the time of the deliberation that the true extent of each arbitrator's independence and impartiality comes to light.

One thing is, in fact, that an arbitrator acts to ensure that the tribunal properly understands the case advanced by his appointed party, which is a totally legitimate conduct I believe, and a different thing is that he acts as an advocate of that party. For purposes of my presentation I will assume that the arbitrator acts in the process of the deliberation in a fair and unbiased manner, leaving the pathological cases to Panel 2.

The exchange of views on the issues to be decided, which is the essence of the deliberation process, takes place in the most varied ways and at different times depending on the specificity of the case, the complexity of the case and the time availability of the arbitrators. We all know that international arbitrators are most of the time located in different places far away from one another and maybe there are other relevant factors. There are, therefore, no best practices, in my view, valid for all international arbitration cases.

As practical experience indicates, there is not just one point in time at which the deliberation process begins: the so-called *mise en délibéré* of the French Code of Civil Procedure. Since as a rule the initiative of the deliberation or the dialogue among arbitrators is left to the chairman, it will depend in most cases on the perception the chairman has acquired of the actual level of independence of his co-arbitrators and, more than that, on the actual level of knowledge each of them has acquired of the case.

The dialogue within the tribunal may start relatively early in a quite open way if the three arbitrators happen to know each other by reason maybe of prior arbitration experience. In the absence of this confidence, the chairman should act with caution. I remember one case in which, maybe younger as I was with less experience probably, during a pause at lunch time of a hearing I started trying to see what were the attitudes and perceptions of my co-arbitrators about the case which was being unfolded in the hearing by observing that maybe one of the parties, a counsel, could have presented an argument rather than what had been said before the tribunal which, in my view, made more sense, and when the hearing was resumed that argument was proposed by the counsel of that party. I discovered that my fellow arbitrator was after all not so independent. This is a warning to behave as chairman with caution, not to advance too early the position he may have on a given case but wait for better knowledge of his colleagues.

Normally the dialogue among arbitrators may start on the eve of an evidentiary hearing when the arbitrators happen to meet in person for the hearing and maybe a good point in time in which to review the content and what will be said at the hearing and prepare a few questions for the witnesses and the experts to be heard. This will allow a very preliminary exchange of views among arbitrators about the case that is being presented before them.

The dialogue may start and continue during the various pauses of the hearing. Coffee breaks are sometimes just designed to permit the arbitrators to have some dialogue among them to see how to develop the hearing which is being conducted. They may on that occasion prepare questions for the parties to be answered in a short time after the hearing or in the context of post-hearing briefs.

It is important, in my view, that whatever the time chosen for discussing the case the chairman should not press his co-arbitrators to reach a quick decision on all issues, advising them rather that the exchange of views is for the time being provisional.

There will be, however, a time at which the arbitrators must reach a decision also to respect time limits which may be prescribed by the applicable rules for rendering an award or, in any case, to abide by the rule whereby the tribunal must avoid unnecessary delays. In my experience, which probably is shared by some of you, the deliberation process continues even during the drafting of the award. It appears sometimes that when you try to write down what was decided during the deliberation process you may discover that it does not work and that you have to re-think it.

Who should go first? As a rule it is the chairman who takes the initiative when he believes that the time is right for initiating examination of an issue to be decided. The best is for the chairman to prepare a kind of check list of questions for each of the issues to be examined based on the parties' arguments regarding each issue and outlining possible alternative solutions to individual issues so as to permit a full discussion.

The preference would be for an open and frank discussion regarding each question leaving initially time for each arbitrator to express his view. Only when the chairman perceives that each arbitrator has stated his position in what, at that point in time, might be considered as a final position then the chairman may intervene and express his position.

Why am I saying that it will be more convenient for the chairman to speak the last during the deliberation process? This is to avoid that by expressing initially his position on individual issues the debate would be confined to less important aspects, even become meaningless, each co-arbitrator joining the chairman's position whenever the views coincide thus forming a majority.

To refer to another situation I experienced, I was an arbitrator with a chairman, a famous Italian law professor, who was a Neapolitan. He started the deliberation process by simply saying: "Dear colleagues we have to decide who is the rascal who should be the losing party in this context." He did not limit himself to posing this question but advanced immediately his own views in a very final determined way. It was a very nice introduction but rather frustrating position for the other arbitrators.

In another case there was another, at least for me, frustrating situation in which the chairman came to the initial deliberation process with a draft of a complete award already prepared. I felt it was a kind of mis-consideration for the position of his co-arbitrators because if you spend time to draft an award it will be difficult to change and redraft what you assume to have carefully drafted.

The fact that the arbitrators must meet physically does not mean that they have in all cases to be there present. There might be deliberations conducted by video conference or telephone. A simple way of starting the deliberation process is for the chairman to prepare a check list, to send the check list to his co-arbitrators, to ask for a reply within a reasonable time limit, to have a second round of exchange of written expressions of views by each arbitrator and then at that point of time the chairman may intervene and express his own views on the various issues.

One final point before I conclude: compromise within the tribunal which I think will be dealt with more in Panel 2. Compromise is in principle to be avoided as a factor weakening, in my opinion, the force of the award and negatively affecting what should be the tribunal's common objective: a coherent and well-reasoned award. Even if a unanimous decision is to be favoured, for obvious reasons to give more strength to an award, this should not be at the price of compromise or concession within the tribunal on the most important aspects of the case. Obviously compromises may be acceptable if there is an objective difficulty in expressing a final view on an individual point, especially on points of law. There might be a genuine uncertainty by an arbitrator what should be the right solution. In that case compromising, in my view, is an acceptable solution.

As we all know, depending on the *lex arbitri* in case of difficulties among the arbitrators to reach a majority, the chairman may act alone but this depends on the applicable rules. Why this provision has been designed by a certain system of law, like the umpire in the English system, is simply to avoid horse trading within the tribunal. Again, if the majority is formed there is no reason to reach unanimity at all costs to favour the minority arbitrator just to have him join the other two arbitrators. The real case for compromise is when there is a genuine irreconcilable disagreement on certain issues among the three arbitrators and the chairman has no power under the applicable rules to decide alone. This I believe is a case for Panel 2. Thank you.

JULIAN LEW:

We now turn to David W. Rivkin.

Form of Deliberations

David W. Rivkin

DAVID W. RIVKIN:
My thesis is that the black box should be as open as possible, as shown in Bernhard's last slide. I think that the earlier and more often the arbitrators can discuss the issues, the better it will be for the process for building a consensus around a final award but also for shaping the process to be the most appropriate for the case. That also means that in appropriate ways and at appropriate times, the parties should understand the issues as the arbitrators are then seeing them, so that concerns can be met and the process can be focused on the issues that are most important to the deliberations and to the final award.

I say this whether I am wearing my hat as counsel for a party or my hat as arbitrator. As counsel for a party, I want to hear from the arbitrators what their thinking is, what their reactions are to the evidence and the arguments made, so that I can make sure I am addressing any particular concerns they have and also so that I do not present them with information or argument that will be unnecessary to their deliberations. As arbitrator, it leads to a more efficient process. I think it helps eventually gain unanimity and comfort among everyone involved.

I think that deliberations in some sense — not deliberations on the final result of course, but deliberations about the issues and how the arbitrators see the case unfolding, deliberations about where the focus of evidence and argument should be — that type of deliberation should begin as early as possible, including at the procedural conference. This is one reason why an in-person procedural conference, even if it means travel, even if it means time away, will often be much more effective than doing a relatively short telephone conference that simply sets procedures going forward. If you are together, if the arbitrators have read the papers that have already been submitted, if they can begin thinking about the types of issues they are going to have to decide and what the parties are going to present to them, it will help them shape the procedure that is appropriate to that case.

Having that kind of dialogue early on is also very important to begin to bind the tribunal together, to begin for the tribunal to work as a unit and not as three individuals. I think that is true, Piero, not only when the arbitrators already know each other, as you said, but also when they do not, because the sooner they begin talking and understanding each other, the sooner trust will develop. At the same time, if you have an arbitrator who is not going to act in an independent and impartial way, such as the situation you described with the lunch time conversation, it is frankly better to know that sooner rather than later, because you can deal with it in the course of the proceedings or at least it helps you put in context whatever you may hear from that arbitrator going forward.

Discussing what the issues are, how they might be approached, what you think the most important type of evidence is going to be, is important at that early stage. Again, I am using deliberations in a broader sense. I am not saying that the arbitrators should show up at a procedural conference and say "Here is how we think this case ought to come out," but they should be talking about the issues in the broader sense of what should be presented.

As procedural issues arise during the case, whether in disputes over requests for documents or interim measures or anti-suit injunctions or any other issues that might arise, there are more opportunities for the arbitrators to deliberate, and they should do so.

Then we get to the hearing stage. I am a firm believer in what I think is called the Reed Retreat: namely, the arbitrators setting aside a day before the hearing to talk about the case and to talk about what they have seen and how the oral hearing might proceed. Again, I think for anyone who is uncomfortable about arbitrators expressing views at that point, you have to focus on the nature of the international arbitration procedure that we follow. Effectively, by the time the parties and the arbitrators arrive for the oral hearing, there has already been phase one of the hearing: a written phase. Parties have submitted testimony and exhibits, and they have submitted arguments. There has already been a hearing, and any arbitrator who has not begun to form an opinion based upon that first phase of the hearing, frankly, I think is not doing his or her job and is not reading the documents as thoroughly and carefully as one ought to do.

Given that, it is perfectly appropriate for the arbitrators to begin to discuss their views based on the evidence and the arguments they have already seen. Those conversations should always be prefaced by statements like "Based on what I have seen, here is where I come out" or "I will be interested in hearing more evidence on this because it may or may not change my view", and so on. The views are still preliminary because phase two of the hearing, the oral phase, has not taken place, but I do think that it would help to be more transparent.

Not only does it help the arbitrators then focus the oral phase of the hearing on the issues that are going to be most important to their decision making, but it also makes the hearing more important from a parties' perspective. It gives me greater confidence that the arbitrators will show up having read the papers as thoroughly as they ought, because I will know they will have had to discuss the papers with the other arbitrators before they arrive at the hearing.

Again, I do not have any concern about pre-judging in these circumstances because the parties have had a very full opportunity to present a lot of their case. Also I think the arbitrators should, where appropriate, give the parties some indication as to what they see as critical issues. If there are issues they want the parties to address, if they have concern about one party's case in a particular area, I do not see any problem with indicating it at that stage. It can be done in a very preliminary way, as an arbitrator and a panel can say, "Based on what we have read so far, we wonder if you will adequately be able to prove X or whether this legal issue might overwhelm the evidence on that particular point."

As a party, I want arbitrators to do that, because it will allow me to focus my evidence and arguments at the oral phase of the hearing in a way that is going to be most useful to them. That kind of interaction all along is very important. For the arbitrators to have those kinds of discussions early on, from the procedural conference to the day before the hearing begins—and if you cannot meet the full day before, at least perhaps dinner the night before—allows them to start fleshing out the case and to develop trust among the panel.

I would not favour arbitrators exchanging their views in writing prior to the hearing, because when you put your views in writing, you cannot flavour it with the provisionality that I was talking about: "Based on what I have seen". It tends to lock arbitrators into positions, and they may come off sounding more like an advocate than they really mean.

During the hearing, I think the arbitrators ought to continue to share reactions and ask appropriate questions of the parties. If the parties do not seem to be focused on the right issues, it is particularly important for the tribunal to intervene and to let them know. When the parties seem to be ships passing in the night, as I have seen in some cases, it is particularly important.

In one ICC case that I chaired recently, the pre-hearing submissions were quite divergent in terms of the way they approached the case, and they did not respond to one another even though there had been two rounds of pre-hearing submissions. Before the opening, the arbitrators talked, and we let the parties know about our concern in that regard and attempted to focus the parties during their openings on those issues. Then when we reached the final stage, we actually provided them with a list of issues to which we wanted them to respond in the post-hearing briefs. We essentially gave them a decision tree to follow, because they were still approaching the case in very different ways.

Another advantage to having this kind of regular dialogue, with the trust that it builds, is that if you do eventually find that one of the arbitrators simply disagrees with the majority view on one or more issues, you can deal with that dissent in a much more appropriate way.

In a different ICC case, we had very good discussions. We had a panel that had worked very well together, but in the end one of the arbitrators simply had a different view as to how the damages ought to be calculated. Because we had the trust, because we had all seen how we approached the case, and because that arbitrator felt that, while he disagreed, he understood the positions that the other two of us were taking, he agreed to put that dissenting view simply in a footnote at the appropriate point of an opinion rather than writing a long and difficult dissent. Again, that was better for the parties.

Let me add that deliberations at the end ought to take place immediately upon the close of the hearing. The arbitrators are in the same place, and the evidence is fresh. I am very unhappy if I am representing a party and I find that the arbitrators are not going to get together until two or three months after the hearing. I feel that the strength of the testimony that I have presented at the hearing may very well get lost in that time.

As those of you who have read the Debevoise Protocol know, I do not believe in full pre-hearing briefs. I think they are a waste of time and effort. Arbitrators ought to focus, if there are going to be post-hearing briefs at all, on the issues and the evidence they really need to know in order to come to their decision. That means the arbitrators need to have done some deliberation. Very often, when I am an arbitrator, I will say to the parties there may very well be post-hearing briefs but we will let you know in a week what issues you can cover. That will give the arbitrators the time to meet the next day to discuss those issues and to be able to focus the post-hearing submissions on what is needed.

In one case, we took an even more extreme action. By the end of the hearing, it was quite clear we were going to rule for the respondent; we thought both the law and the facts dictated that. The claimant wanted to present a post-hearing brief, so we did some initial deliberating while the parties were still present. We came back and said to the claimant: you wish to submit a post-hearing brief, we would like you to do so by this particular date, please present all of the arguments that you think we need to consider in order to rule in your favour. I said we will then deliberate and, if we believe a post-hearing brief by the respondent is necessary, we will inform it within two weeks after the submission of the first brief and then set up an appropriate deadline for that brief.

This direction gave a clear signal to the parties of what we then believed. We had heard the evidence, and it was appropriate for us to do so. Asking the respondent to submit a brief that we did not need, which would have cost that party a quarter of a million dollars in additional time, simply would not have been appropriate in that case. That is perhaps an extreme version but one we thought was appropriate.

To conclude, deliberating early and often, and holding the final deliberation on the merits immediately upon the close of the hearing, is very important. Thank you.

Drafting the Award

Matthias Scherer

MATTHIAS SCHERER:

We have heard from Piero Bernardini and David W. Rivkin the form of deliberations, the organisation of the deliberations so my task is to go beyond the deliberations to the stage where the arbitrators have reached a decision, or think they have reached a decision, but the award is not yet drafted. I will not deal with arbitrators who have second thoughts at that stage, although I should mention a most remarkable experience I had when after the very first deliberation one of the arbitrators sent straight away his dissenting opinion to the ICC, and at that stage the award had not been written. At least he made himself clear.

It is very important that at the deliberations decisions are actually reached. We all know the situation, especially over a good lunch or dinner, no-one is very contentious and maybe there are things left open but once you start drafting the award you realise that although you thought you came out of the deliberation with a decision it is something completely else to fine tune it and to put in a written form. The chairman should always make sure, and also the co-arbitrators, that decisions are actually taken at the deliberation.

Who should draft the award? In my view this is the task and the prerogative of the chairman although there may be exceptions, for instance if the applicable law is not one in which the chairperson is qualified. In that event he may ask one of the co-arbitrators who is qualified in that law to prepare notes or to provide further drafts of relevant sections. It is usually not advisable to have collective drafting especially if the linguistic skills of the arbitrators are not identical because then you see from the award who has written it and also who has not written the relevant sections, which may give the wrong impression to the reader.

Suggestions from the chair that a co-arbitrator should write certain sections are usually met with more enthusiasm if the arbitrators are paid by the hour rather than the normal ICC way of allotting fees which is more 40/30/30.

What about the form of the award? The deliberations are the start but you have to come up with an award which needs to meet the form at the place of arbitration. In Switzerland we have Article 189 of the PIL Act: the award shall be made in accordance with the parties' agreements and if no such agreement exists the award is to be in writing, it has to have reasons, it has to carry a date and the signatures of the arbitrators but the signature of the chairman is sufficient. You may find and actually have to look for further guidance on the form of the award in the applicable arbitration rules and/or in the *lex arbitri* at the place of arbitration.

In the binder you will find the ICC check list for the drafting of an award which has a caption in a box that it is not mandatory, et cetera, but everyone who has written an award for the ICC recently will know that it is applied very strictly. The ICC will draw your attention to any mistake or omission you may have committed. I find it quite well done actually because even experienced arbitrators sometimes forget nuts and bolts and dots on "i"s which should be there.

As to the signature of the award, I will not speak again about the dissenting arbitrator and those who do not want to sign but about more practical aspects. Especially if there are time lines applicable one should make sure that the arbitrators are available to sign. For the award real signatures are required, not electronic ones. Absence of arbitrators due to vacations or otherwise may be a problem so the signature gathering process has to be organised at an early stage.

Is the place of signature relevant? In Switzerland it is not. There is case law on that, a Supreme Court decision of 24 March 1997, ASA Bulletin 1997, page 360: the award is deemed to be made at the place of arbitration. This is also the formula of the ICC how they want you to sign the arbitral award in order to avoid confusions because in certain *lex arbitri* there may be confusion about the place of arbitration and the place of signature and at the enforcement stage that might be a problem.

One issue that comes up quite often during the drafting of the award is whether the arbitral tribunal should speak about the law, give reasons or explain the law. Clearly the answer should be yes, and also Bernhard Berger mentioned it in his opening speech. Bernhard referred to it as an obligation (duty to apply the law). Maybe it is not an obligation but it is certainly good practice so the parties and their lawyers can understand where the tribunal was persuaded and where it was not persuaded.

A more interesting question is whether a tribunal can rely on legal authorities that were not mentioned by the parties: whether they can, whether they should, whether they must rely on such authorities. I think in Switzerland they can rely, subject only to the rule *jura novit curia*, the right to be heard, and the prohibition to take the parties by surprise, which is a very high threshold. Short of something utterly unexpected and unforeseeable for both parties the tribunal can invoke authorities that were not mentioned or raised by the parties.

Should the tribunal do that? That also depends on the quality of the briefs, especially if the law is pleaded by counsel not qualified in the law that is applicable to the merits. Sometimes you have very basic pleadings and the arbitrators have to rely on authorities that have not been pleaded. I thought that this would be possible without problem subject to the provision of taking the parties by surprise but I was told recently that the ICC looks also whether legal authorities in the award have actually been brought up in the underlying arbitration proceedings. This is not my experience. It was a co-arbitrator who mentioned that but it is clear, especially in the common law, parties are expected to plead the case in full and legal authorities should be brought up at an early stage and it is not expected that arbitrators raise such authorities in the award on their own initiative. That may also be a cultural aspect here.

Another more mundane post-deliberation issue is money. *Money* matters or money *matters*; you can pronounce it any way you want. The chairperson should keep an eye on advances paid by the parties and whether there is enough money available to pay for the arbitration, which includes the arbitrators' fees, but not only those, also the court reporters, the hotels. In an arbitration where I am the only Swiss on the panel, I was recently informed by a Geneva hotel that they were not fully paid by the parties for the hearing arrangements. Luckily this problem could be resolved in time before the award was issued. The arbitral tribunal cannot in its award order the parties to pay a third party service provider just as they cannot order the parties to pay their own fees. This is also a well-known Swiss case law so this has to be done and dealt with when drafting the award.

Arbitrators should also be wary if the chairman starts telling anecdotes about co-arbitrators who have come up with outrageous figures of hours they have spent on the case because usually that is the first step in making a proposal on a different split of the fees than 40/30/30.

You should take note of these anecdotes though, so you can make use of them if you are in the chair the next time!

The ICC may, if on its face the arbitrators have spent considerably less time than others, on their own motion change the allocation of fees among on the arbitrators.

VAT is also an issue to be considered when drafting the award. There may be VAT liabilities of certain arbitrators who have to be taken care of.

Time limits for issuing the award, there are certain arbitration agreements that provide for time limits. These have to be very carefully studied by the arbitral tribunal so they can issue their award in due time. I would mention a Swiss case which is published in ASA Bulletin 2006, p. 125, where an award was enforced in Switzerland and one party said it was rendered late. This was not upheld because the party had not shown when the triggering date actually was and the triggering date was the start of the deliberations. This shows that sometimes deliberations can be an important timing factor.

The excessive length of the deliberations can be a denial of justice. There is a Swiss Supreme Court case 5P.292/2005 which addressed a number of issues under the New York Convention, including delay. The arbitration went on for seven years and the award was issued one year after the last steps in the proceedings. The Swiss Supreme Court found that this was not a denial of justice. I am currently waiting for an ICSID award which has been three years since the hearing. I would not know how this would be qualified but certainly it is not just a standard practice (in the meantime rendered: Rompetrol v Romania).

My time is up but I had one final point, service of the award, which is something the tribunal should consider. May I refer you to a very well written paper by Hans van Houtte, *The Delivery of Awards to Parties,* which is in Arbitration International 2005. Thank you.

JULIAN LEW:

I am not sure what the role of the moderator is. Is it to try to sum up what you have already heard? I could try to do that but not as eloquently or as completely as any of our three speakers so I am reluctant to do that. Is it to be that of a chairman, which is to express his own views over what one has heard from everybody else? I do not propose to do that either. What I would rather do is to invite your views and your ideas of what you have heard but with perhaps a little bit of guidance from me trying to channel the ideas while bringing together some of the concepts that we have heard.

Before I introduce that, can I ask you, and repeating again what you heard earlier from Michael E. Schneider, when you wish to speak please wait for the microphone because it is recorded. Many people here will know one another but for the record could you introduce yourself and your name. Could I also ask you to keep your comments short, to a maximum of two minutes, so other people will have an opportunity to participate.

There was a slight discrepancy in the way the point of deliberations was presented by both Piero and David a bit earlier. The question of when the deliberations should commence, and I will move on from that, let me ask this question to start. If at an early stage the arbitrators have reached a view or had a discussion and they do not feel that the parties are with them, the ships crossing in the night that David identified, do you think that this would be an appropriate time for arbitrators to give an indication to the parties what the tribunal would like to hear, asking them to address specific points, perhaps even having a hearing just on a specific issue? Should they give an indication where one particular question might be determinative of the case? Of course if they deal with that in isolation one party may feel that is somewhat to their prejudice. Let me put that out to the audience and we would welcome your comments.

CHRISTOPH LIEBSCHER:

I am very much in favour of the approach of David. To answer your question personally, I would be cautious and in doubt ask the parties whether they agree for the tribunal to disclose part of their brains to the parties. There may be situations, as you described, of passing ships where I personally would tend to address that because I would want to make clear that we are not on the same boat yet. Otherwise, I would be pretty cautious and in general terms ask the parties' counsel whether they are fine with the arbitral tribunal sharing their views.

One question I may suggest which is in my mind is the issue of re-opening when during deliberations you may find that there is reason to do so. I would be interested in the views of the very experienced panel members if that could or should occur?

CRENGUTA LEAUA:

I would like to highlight a certain possible view on the issue of the dissenting opinions. That view would bring into discussion the role of the arbitrators in specific law areas, like for instance in international public law. In this area, the opinions of the arbitrators are usually much more frequently made public than in commercial arbitration. They have a role in building certain types of arguments and they construct in time the jurisprudence. Therefore, they contribute to the legal doctrine. In these cases, I can see — and I would like also to see whether the distinguished members of the panel may have some comment on that — a thin line, between, on one hand, the secrecy of the deliberations and the point that was brought into discussion in the early phase of this conference in the morning on rather encouraging not to draft dissenting opinions than encouraging drafting such dissenting opinions and, on the other hand, the possibility of giving to the legal community some food for thought and to show that maybe the majority opinion in a certain arbitral tribunal is not the only opinion that may be later on used by the international community in order to argue certain arguments.

Particularly in ICSID arbitrations I saw that dissenting opinions are sometimes very interesting. In time there may be a certain evolution into which one is the majority opinion and which one may be the minority opinion, like for instance the definition of the investor or others.

DAVID LAWSON:

I hate and hesitate to disagree with my dear colleague David W. Rivkin but I would have been a very unhappy camper if I was the respondent's counsel in the extreme case that you said.

DAVID W. RIVKIN:

Not if you were the claimant's counsel.

DAVID LAWSON:

If I understand correctly the tribunal was leaning pretty strongly to the claimant's position.

DAVID W. RIVKIN:

No, the other way around.

DAVID LAWSON:

So you are allowing the party not doing well to make their submission.

DAVID W. RIVKIN:

Yes.

DAVID LAWSON:

I misunderstood you.

DAVID W. RIVKIN:

To be clear, it was the claimant's position we thought would not succeed. The claimant wanted to make a submission so we gave the claimant one more opportunity to try to convince us we were wrong.

If the claimant did not succeed with its post-hearing brief, then there was no reason for the respondent also to waste time and money on a post-hearing.

DAVID LAWSON:

If I was respondent's counsel in that case and I was confident I might go along with it without being too upset but I have guessed wrongly how a tribunal is leaning in a case before and I would much rather have the opportunity to put my last word in whichever side I am on.

DAVID W. RIVKIN:

So it is clear, we were prepared to rule against the claimant. We wanted to give the claimant one more opportunity to be heard which the claimant took advantage of. What we said is if the claimant failed to convince us after that brief, then there is no need for another brief by the respondent. If the claimant raised some issues we had not considered or changed our mind, then of course we would have let the respondent have the last word so each of them would have submitted a post-hearing brief. Neither of them would have been denied the opportunity to be heard, but there is no need for the respondent to give us a brief telling us what we were already going to decide if that was the point we got to after reading the claimant's brief.

JULIAN LEW:

This is quite a controversial issue as to whether you should give somebody who has already had the opportunity to put their case and there are two very distinct views which is the best way to go.

NATHALIE VOSER:

I do not have a problem with this approach because that is how the Swiss Supreme Court would do it: if they rule in favour of a party there is no need to be heard by the party in whose favour they ruled. I have another problem, David, with what you said in terms of giving the parties the heads-up on where you stand.

We are more and more moving to an inquisitorial system which in terms of efficiency I am fully in favour because it is very efficient but it tends to blur the burden of proof. I am in favour of asking the counsel a leading question regarding legal issues because I think that regarding the law it is not about who brings in the argument if the argument is right but when it comes to issues of fact I realise more and more arbitrators are not concerned any more about who bears the burden of proof. If you start talking to the parties "I would like to hear more about these factual issues", are you not unduly assisting the party who bears the burden of proof? Should you not more rely on what is in the file and tough luck to the parties not well represented who did not bring up the essential factual issues? I think that is a very delicate problem because it could be an unequal treatment to the party who does not bear the burden of proof.

JULIAN LEW:

I will take a few more comments and then ask the three panellists to comment on those issues.

DAVID HACKING:

In the last of these excellent ASA conferences I attended I introduced an old English proverb. I was highly complimented because speaker after speaker adopted that ancient English proverb until to the last speaker, who was a very learned and intelligent English High Court judge, who said he had never heard of it. I will, therefore, introduce to this programme, with some nervousness, another ancient English proverb. I should mention that the proverb I introduced three years ago, on the issue of whether arbitral tribunals should be seeking the truth, was: "Truth is the daughter of time". The proverb I introduce to this programme is: "Beware of the demons in the black box."

I have to say that introducing this further ancient proverb I do so with a great deal of nervousness on what Julian is going to say about it or Phillip Capper who are the three representatives from London.

Therefore, I move to congratulate David W. Rivkin on his bravery because he started his address to us that the black box should be as open as possible and I thoroughly agree with his views about the dialogue between the tribunal and counsel.

PIERRE-ANDRÉ MORAND:

I would raise again the matter of the dissenting opinion. It is always an unpleasant situation where in a decision by arbitrators there is one of them feeling obliged to express a dissenting view. I feel that there is another way to deal with this situation. It is said there could be a footnote on the dissenting opinion but in most cases a footnote is too short to express the view of a dissenting arbitrator. A practical way would be to include the views of the dissenting arbitrator in the award starting by saying the arbitral tribunal has considered a situation, which is the dissenting opinion of this arbitrator, and in the end saying finally it did not adopt these views so the dissenting opinion is, in fact, included in the award.

KIRSTIN DODGE:

I wanted to raise some questions to David W. Rivkin about the idea of having main deliberations immediately post the oral hearing. I worry that it overemphasises witness evidence as opposed to the documentary evidence. I worry that arbitrators do not come to the oral cross-examination hearing really having studied the file. I would be curious of the feedback from the panel members and the experiences in that regard because this entirely determines, from an advocate's perspective, what you want to be doing at the oral hearing. Does that mean we are moving to week long or two-week hearings with full opening arguments, with full closing arguments, with Livenote? Of course we think as advocates that cross-examination matters but it will not necessarily be obvious until you pull the documents together with the testimony, compared to witness statements and you pull the package together. Can we do that in a week, in two days or should we even try? I am totally open but it depends on how prepared the arbitrators are and if that is going to be the main and last opportunity.

ANDREAS REINER:

Honestly, I would be reluctant, particularly in a rather fact-driven case, to start deliberating immediately after the hearing. I think you need time to reflect on what you have heard. You may want to go through the transcript of the hearing. I think it does not give the right impression to the parties. Is it not part of the right to be heard of the parties to have an opportunity to present their case and to say what they take out of the evidence that has been presented?

I can understand your approach if the case is very law driven. On legal issues which you may have read and considered beforehand, you can deliberate immediately thereafter. But, when you have had a hearing of three, four or five days are you really in a position to immediately jump to a conclusion on factual issues? Even if you tell the parties, "I have, of course, an open mind. You submit your post-hearing brief. I can change my mind and then I will ask the other party as well", I think the impression that is left with the parties may be pretty unfortunate. It depends on the circumstances but as a general rule I would avoid that type of situation.

Secondly, I do agree that there is very often a lack of communication between the arbitrators and the parties. It is a very delicate issue. In a certain number of cases I have tried to persuade the parties when we put together the time line of the arbitration and I said should we not meet after the first round of submissions and see what we think about that case, what are the legal issues, what are the factual issues? I fully agree with the danger of whether you get involved in burden of proof issues but I did not encounter a great enthusiasm from the parties. In fact, you have a case that goes on for perhaps a year, sometimes more, with four submissions and then only you meet for the first time with the arbitrators.

The question is would it not be more efficient if you leave some time for the arbitrators after the first round of submissions so that they can get together. I think it would make sense for them to meet in person. You cannot do it by telephone or by written exchange of views.

When you start deliberations early on, which I think is perfectly fine, what do you do with that? It only makes sense if it helps you to properly prepare the hearing by putting together a list of questions that you want to put to the parties or the experts and to the witnesses, otherwise starting discussing a case without drawing any benefit from that I think that is just nonsense. The only possibility is that you fix your mind without any benefit to the case. Why do that?

I am certainly not saying that the co-arbitrator was right in making sure that that party would raise that issue but I can sense a sort of frustration. Why would arbitrators say in an internal meeting "why do they not make this or that argument?" Either the arbitrators raise the issue openly with the parties to allow the parties to understand and address the point, or not. I do not see the purpose of a tribunal making a point internally and then say nothing to the parties.

RABAB YASEEN:

Considering the potential bias issue we heard from the panel, I would like to ask Matthias how comfortable he would be — as Chairman of the arbitral tribunal unfamiliar with the applicable law — to rely on feedback from a party-appointed co-arbitrator?

JULIAN LEW:

I do not want to keep anybody from their coffee or networking or catching up with old friends, but before we do that I ask our three panellists if they would like to come back. Several very interesting questions have come up but three in particular that have reverberated: one is the dissenting opinions; the other is this question of when you should be deliberating and what to do; and the other is the importance of the post-hearing brief.

PIERO BERNARDINI:

I may answer to a couple of questions on dissenting opinions. Leaving aside the problem of the consistency of dissenting opinion with the secrecy of the deliberation, I would try to draw a distinction between investment treaty arbitration and commercial arbitration. In commercial arbitration my experience is in the sense that the arbitrator who wishes to file and actually files a dissenting opinion most of the time is led by the desire to show to the party who has appointed him that he has done his best and the fault is of that poor majority who has taken a very wrong decision. I would not push too far the other consideration, namely that of offering some arguments to that party to attack the award.

I must say I never find myself in a minority position. I do not know why, not necessarily because I am a very convincing lawyer! I would favour a solution according to which the award should clearly state that on a certain decision only the majority was in agreement and there was evidently one minority arbitrator without having a dissenting opinion. As we know, neither the ICC Court nor any other institution considers a dissenting opinion at any point in time as something which might affect the value of the tribunal's work.

Investment treaty arbitration might be different. There is experience, which in a way is drawn from the International Court of Justice, of dissenting or concurring opinion as a means of advancing the law. Considering the authority of the arbitrator at that level a dissenting opinion may really help in better understanding the development of the law. In my experience as an arbitrator in investment treaty arbitration even seeing parties in their pleadings referring to dissenting opinions as a kind of authority to support their individual positions.

DAVID W. RIVKIN:

Thanks for all the comments. I certainly agree with what Christoph said about asking for the permission of the parties if you are going to give some preliminary views. I do not think simply asking questions and focussing the parties in their presentation raises the same issue, but if you are really going to give some preliminary views, you need to do that. That is one of the advantages to having the arbitrators talk about the issues at an early stage. I have had cases where I have acted in a very Swiss German way and, at an appropriate time during a hearing or at the close of the hearing before briefing, have asked the parties if the Tribunal could give some preliminary views that we thought might help work towards a settlement. The parties have always accepted the suggestion, and have found the comments to be useful. That approach can be helpful, but you have to be careful to do it with the permission of the parties.

I completely agree with Nathalie's comment on the burden of proof. I do not think there is necessarily a conflict between raising issues or focusing the parties and ignoring the burden of proof that one party has. I think it has to be done carefully.

In terms of the immediate deliberation and the points that were made, I am assuming that the arbitrators have read the relevant documents before the hearing and that the arbitrators now have effectively sat through two phases of the hearing: one written and one oral. By saying I think it is important to meet immediately does not mean that you necessarily have to come to a final decision that day but meeting immediately, understanding where there is agreement and where you may need to go back and look at the documents again, look at the testimony again, look at the law again, so that you can then continue your deliberations, is very helpful. Simply waiting some period of time is not going to help that process because then, when you get back together, you still have to do that a second time. I do think the parties have a right to a prompt award as well.

I simply adopt what Piero said on dissenting opinions.

MATTHIAS SCHERER:

Nathalie's point about the burden of proof and giving hints from the tribunal, I think that can be a problem. The problem is different if you act as counsel or as arbitrator. As counsel I share these concerns; as an arbitrator may be less because as an arbitrator one has to draft the award. For me it is difficult to say "Tough luck, they have not seen it. Burden of proof." I think some decisions have to be made but I never thought of that and I think I will do so more in the future.

As to the question whether I feel comfortable with another arbitrator writing part of the law if I am not familiar with it, no I am not. I would try to find out more about it especially if he is biased. Usually biased arbitrators focus on the bias and not on being good at providing law and then will probably want to focus on the contract rather than on the law.

Andreas Reiner's comment about not deliberating after the hearing I share sometimes, sometimes not. If the tribunal is well prepared, as it should be but one should not assume that they are, they come out in the hearing already with some ideas about what the relevant issues are. This was Kirstin Dodge's concerns about the overemphasis on witness statements. The arbitrators should always be familiar with the main factual issues and, if they are, I think after the hearing can be a good moment to deliberate but I think it is a case-by-case decision. Especially if there are biased arbitrators and you can feel that, I think it is not good to deliberate. It is better let them go, take their planes and do it afterwards.

JULIAN LEW:

In the traditional English way I would say that I have listened to what the panel has had to say, I have plenty I would like to add but nothing I am going to add. I would like to commend ASA and Bernhard Berger for this subject. The way the discussion has gone shows how important and interesting it is. On that basis I hope we have if not opened at least put a little hole into the black box of the way some people think.

Finally, I would like to thank our three panellists who have really enlightened us greatly today and got this conference off to a firm start. I wish you well for the rest of today's deliberations.

Panel 2

Conflict in the Deliberations: Dealing with Bias and Obstruction

Moderated by Markus Wirth

BERNHARD BERGER:

Panel 2 is about conflicts in deliberations. It will particularly also cover the dissenting opinions that have caught much attention already this morning. Panel 2 is chaired by Markus Wirth. I do not have to introduce him to this audience as our immediate past-president of ASA.

MARKUS WIRTH:

First of all, please excuse my voice; it is the remnant of the flu but since this is the show of my co-panellists much more than mine that should not be a problem.

I am pleased to introduce Panel 2 and particularly the topic of Panel 2. As far as the panellists are concerned, I would like to refer you to their detailed CVs which you will find in the conference binder. Generally what Julian has said with respect to the composition of Panel 1 applies one to one to this panel. We have a richness of experience here on this panel in terms of legal background and variety of legal activity, academic and as practitioners: we have Phillip Capper representing the common law view; we have Pierre Mayer from Paris; and we have Bernhard Meyer from Zurich.

When I look at their CVs and add the cases I had with my colleagues up here, I think we can profit from a combined experience gathered in several hundred deliberations. That promises, hopefully, to provide a very interesting discussion of our topic.

The topic is conflict in the deliberations: dealing with bias and obstruction. How will we go about it? We divided the topic into three sub-topics. The first sub-topic is how to deal with bias and obstruction: what are the typical situations of arbitrators' misconduct, bias or obstruction, how to react to such situations and, as a further issue, should misconduct, excessive bias and/or obstruction be reported and, if yes, when, by whom and to whom?

The second sub-topic is the bargaining process among the arbitrators. Although Piero Bernardini has emphasised that the aim of the arbitrators is to reach a correct decision reflecting properly the law and of course the facts, it is a fact that cannot be denied, in my view, that deliberations to a large extent include a bargaining process among the arbitrators. Ugo Draetta, in his recent most interesting book *Behind the Scenes of International Arbitration*, has stated, talking about the arbitrators and in particular the co-arbitrators: "The better their negotiating skills the better the results arbitrators achieve in deliberations."

It is a sensitive issue but we intend to address it.

In the framework of that topic various questions come up: should a bargaining process at all be attempted, i.e. a sort of embracing approach, embracing the views of all the three arbitrators, opposed to an antagonistic approach? Secondly, if there is a bargaining process, what are the available bargaining chips, for instance a concession on quantum in return for a unanimous decision on liability? What kind of bargaining chip does the cost decision provide to the arbitrators? Generally: what should be the goal of the chairman? Should it be to reach a unanimous decision or should it be to reach what he or she thinks is the right decision?

The third sub-topic we want to address is the dissenting opinion. That topic has already been addressed by the first panel but we may wish to add some practical aspects to the discussion: how to structure a dissenting opinion; in what form do you want to communicate it to the parties; and who should have the authority to disclose dissenting opinions to the parties. These are the issues that are of concern to us in our daily practice.

We will proceed as follows: Phillip Capper will introduce how to deal with bias and obstruction. I will then provide my co-panellists with an opportunity to react to his remarks or add some experiences of their own and after that we would like to have a brief question and answer round with the audience with respect to the first sub-topic. We will then proceed the same way regarding the second and third sub-topics. The second sub-topic will be introduced by Bernhard Meyer: structuring the bargaining process. The third sub-topic will be introduced by Pierre Mayer: dissenting opinions.

Dealing with Bias and Obstruction

Phillip Capper

PHILLIP CAPPER:

Thank you very much indeed. It is a great privilege to be invited to be here. It is a particular responsibility to be tarred with the brush of the common law but I will see what I can do with that. It is a real pleasure nevertheless to be here and I am very grateful for this opportunity.

Bias, misconduct and obstruction: what our chairman has not told you but he has told us is that we are to speak about practical experiences, of situations likely to arise in typical arbitration. We have been told not to give you an abstract legal discourse so we will not. These are my experiences and they come from commercial arbitrations rather than from investor protection cases.

I have had some bad experiences. My bad experiences have more commonly been when counsel looking at the tribunal—I mean bad experiences with bad arbitrators when looking as counsel—but nevertheless I want to broaden the idea of bias. Much of what I say has come from my experience as arbitrator. I speak this morning more from my experience as arbitrator than as counsel.

We will have to think about this question of reporting misconduct but that assumes we agree on what is misconduct and I am not sure there are very good channels for the reporting of misconduct in any event.

Bias, what is it: a prejudice, an inclination to prefer one thing over another, one person over another, one group over another, one thing over another; it can be actual or it can be apparent. If it is actual bias then the solution is normally going to be within the secrecy of the arbitral tribunal; it is for the other arbitrators to deal with it. Often it is actual but not apparent. If it is apparent, the parties are going to deal with it and they have plenty of weapons to deal with it during the arbitration or afterwards and in that sense the reporting will be dealt with.

Let us start at the beginning and see what affects deliberations. I am going to emphasise the point that in a sense deliberations carry on all the way through the process, though I am very struck by the point that Andreas Reiner made in a previous session asking what do you do with early deliberations. It seems to me the point of the deliberations coming early is to identify the issues, to identify the real questions, to reduce the issues to be decided and arrive at efficient hearings and potentially even efficient later submissions.

What biases are there? I have identified from actual experience a few and I call them appointment bias, knowledge bias, representational bias, useful bias, party bias which includes issue bias, then I will come to the two that really matter in my view: cultural bias and what I have called case load bias, although you can also call it easy life bias but I will come back to that. I will do all of that in about four minutes.

There is a trend amongst co-arbitrators, especially the experienced ones, to appoint the chair or presiding arbitrator themselves. Parties do not like that so much. Parties today want to be involved in the appointment of the presiding chair and I think we should encourage that. That involves unfortunately some form of *ex parte* communication. Some, particularly English co-arbitrators, are concerned by the idea of *ex parte* communication at that stage. They need to get over it and get real. We need to have involvement of co-arbitrators listening to the parties in appropriate ways in order to arrive at the right presiding arbitrator.

There is a conundrum in this whole idea of bias. The conundrum or paradox is this: we as counsel, especially in the larger law firms like mine, White & Case, spend an enormous amount of effort thinking about the selection of the right arbitrators and I know all other practitioners do the same. Especially the parties — and some of those parties are in this room — who are repeat purchasers of arbitration also go to great lengths to select the right arbitrators. I do not mean for one moment that they intend any kind of bias but they clearly think they are selecting something distinctive. They must believe that there are characteristics in these people selected which are *more* than expeditious, fair minded, intelligent, well qualified available skill sets. If all that is true of good arbitrators, and if that is the correct description of good arbitrators, you may as well just have any of them who are available. What is it that parties and their counsel are seeking? The conundrum is that there must be some expectation in selecting and appointing arbitrators, that there is some characteristic present. I want to come back to some of those characteristics because one person's characteristic is another person's bias.

Knowledge bias. I had this where one of the co-arbitrators where I was chairing the tribunal clearly knew a lot about the context. He knew about the sector, he knew about the region, he knew about the realities of life in relation to our subject matter. That was easy to deal with. We made very sure that if in so far as his knowledge was relevant and the points he was raising were appropriate they were exposed to the parties early and there was no question of it affecting us in a way which the parties had not been able to address.

My worst ever deliberation was what I call a reputational bias case. I was sitting as chairman with a distinguished English QC as one of my co-arbitrators. The case had been won ultimately outright by one of the parties on very good legal points but the party which had won outright had wasted the tribunal's time and the other party's time by going through a weak jurisdictional challenge which took up months and required a partial award. I and one co-arbitrator were clear: costs depend on the relative success of the parties therefore the party that won overall had to give some account for the wasted costs in the jurisdictional phase.

The QC was indignant. I have never seen a co-arbitrator so angry. "Phillip" he said "if people find out what will they say about me? I must award costs which follow the event. Any good Englishman knows that, don't you?" I explained that the parties had not come to London in order to get English High Court justice but come to London in order to see a good international arbitration and under the rules under which we were deciding it was clear that we had to take into account the relative success of the parties.

How did we deal with it? It was very tough, it was very difficult, we had to negotiate but in the end we succeeded. By reflecting his observations we managed to bring him around on a very carefully crafted element of the award. He was worried that the English courts would think that he did not understand the English rules on costs when sitting as an arbitrator. That was irrelevant to our case and it was a form of bias.

There is useful bias. It may seem more like bias if you have come from a common law tradition west of where I live across a very large pond. That kind of bias is the kind of bias that says any indication that the arbitrators have thought of the matter at all early is a form of bias. It cannot be true, if you come this far east, that to have thought about it is by definition bias.

I remember one tribunal where we sat. We came to the end of the hearing and (contrary to what has been suggested earlier today that it is not a good time to have thought) we thought about things and the chairman came up with a good idea which we two co-arbitrators agreed with: that we would write to the parties even before beginning the process of writing an enormously long award and ask them if they would like to have an early indication and would they agree to accept an early indication, of course with agreement to avoid any question of objection by way of bias. It was useful, it had the prospect of avoiding further proceedings and it seems to me those that think that to be bias is overcome by agreement. It is clearly useful.

Party bias. That is what you thought I was going to talk about and I am not going to say much about it. We all have war stories of people who appear to be biased. What I am more concerned about is what you might call issue bias and that is really difficult in the area of commercial arbitration and talked about a lot in relation to investor protection. Should we be worried about arbitrators who appear to have a view on a given issue?

Let us come quickly to the other two topics which seem to be the most important: cultural bias. I do not have any problem with national cultural bias in the sense that one of the co-arbitrators understands one of the party's cultures and occasionally reminds his or her co-arbitrators what we have to keep in mind. This is not stuff that needs to be exposed. It is just to understand the differences that come from different national characteristics at a very basic level of communication.

The most serious bias in our world of international arbitration is the one we are least aware of. The most serious bias confronting this group of people in this room or any discussion of international arbitration is that unspoken, often unrecognised legal cultural bias; that we bring our formation into the room with us and do not even realise it is there. I have been horrified especially by my co-English arbitrators who have not realised that *the* English solution is simply *an* English solution. They may think it is universal, perfect, objective and to be admired and they are wrong on all counts in some cases. Take, for example, some attitudes to privilege amongst English arbitrators. It is this unspoken, unrealised type of bias which seems to me to be the most significant.

I come to the new trend. I had to give it a title: case load bias I call it but if you are a retired lawyer you might call it easy life bias. Even arbitrators in retirement may not want to waste time reading until they really have to—which is why they may not like Lucy Reed's Reed Retreat. As in the courts, the case may go away, it may settle; why do they need to read documents until they really know the case will hold up?

For the busy professional it comes up all the time. For the "look how many cases they have got on their ICC availability statement" arbitrators, it is a case load bias. Bias is an inclination to prefer one thing over another. They are concerned with the rest of their case load. How do they handle the case?

I know this is a topic for this afternoon but I think there are real difficulties here in the management of arbitration by busy arbitrators by the use of others to assist them in the process. There is a whole topic this afternoon but the bias is: preferring the maintenance of their arbitrator case load than the demands of this case. By taking on this case they have to be prepared, they have to read, they have to know the issues.

MARKUS WIRTH:

That was a very interesting, extensive definition of bias and also a very refreshing one particularly from a common law lawyer! I guess it is well received by this audience.

Next, I would like to invite my co-panellists to react to some issues that Phillip raised or add some of their own experiences in dealing with bias and obstruction.

PIERRE MAYER:

I can only react with admiration as that was fascinating. I can only add a few things and maybe one war story. The subject is obstruction and bias. I have had very little experience fortunately with obstruction, in fact when I think of all the cases I have been in I find only one case, which is original I think. It was an arbitration in Geneva and in the middle of the first meeting, which was important, one of the arbitrators left the room. We told him "You cannot do that. You knew there would be this meeting until 5 pm" and he said "Yes, but I have an appointment in Paris. My train is going to leave soon. I have to leave", and he left. Then we asked ourselves what to do. I was the other co-arbitrator, and the chairman asked the parties would they accept that we continue until the end of this meeting; he of course undertook to inform the arbitrator who has left of what has been said. After some hesitation and reticence they said OK. Then we continued and then we informed the co-arbitrator who had left.

From the point of view of the party whose arbitrator, if I can express myself in that way, had left, it seemed that we had not given him enough information and that our decision was in fact to be set aside. They went to the Tribunal Fédéral who fortunately said no, everything was perfectly correct. I am convinced that there was an agreement between the party and the arbitrator who left to derail the arbitration. That is one example of obstruction.

As to bias, in contrast I have seen bias more often than not, even about what could be called a slight difference. One important question is how to deal with partial arbitrators, whether there is only one who is partial, a co-arbitrator, or both are? That is a problem to be tackled by the chairman.

I think that the best way to arrive at a unanimous award or at least to diminish the inconveniences of bias partially is to start discussing the various aspects of the case rather early on and in an informal way during breaks and lunches. That gives the chairman the opportunity to let the co-arbitrators understand that certain arguments are not likely to convince him. Of course he will not say A is right and B is wrong, of course not; it must be done with tact. It will persuade the partial co-arbitrator that this is not the right way to convince the chairman and he fears that he will lose credibility; in fact, it narrows the issues of disagreement.

I think this progressive and informal way of deliberating is much more efficient than to wait until the end and then have deliberation in a solemn meeting at which the biased co-arbitrators will come to fight as fiercely as they can to convince the chairman not knowing what he thinks. I think it is not a good tactic for a chairman to remain inscrutable to the end of the discussions. That can of course be exclusive. That is what I wanted to add to what Phillip said.

BERNHARD MEYER:

I would like to raise a question, first with the panel and perhaps also with the audience. I have seen biased arbitrators as many of you have too. My experience is that their weight in general is not very great because what happens is that the other two arbitrators, the non-biased arbitrators, rally together and disregard what a biased arbitrator says.

My question to the panellists, and to myself when I get in the situation where the other arbitrator is biased, is, however, what should I do? Should I also start to take very one-sided views, in order to counter-balance the other arbitrator? Shall I do nothing? There is always a danger in an arbitral tribunal, that if one arbitrator is being difficult and biased, the chairman somehow tries to make compromises to get through. All he wants is to get through with the procedure. If you then do not take the opposite view to counter-balance the bias, you may have a problem.

I would like to ask you what do you do in such a situation? Do you stay totally neutral and think the chair will handle this, he/she will notice the bias and correct it; or do you off-set the pressure? What do you do?

PHILLIP CAPPER:

First of all, the chair will speak with that arbitrator alone over the coffee, the dinner and so on; it depends on the context of the arbitration. The kinds of cases I am involved with are typically large infrastructure engineering construction projects so one is not talking about a process to a very short hearing. There are stages before that. There are issues before that.

Concretely, if it comes up in the hearing there are balancing things that the chair can do. The chair can control the clock. The chair can interrupt questioning and encourage the other co-arbitrator to ask some questions, can ask balancing questions. It is dangerous to waste time but can ask, in a sense, unnecessary questions but to keep the balance.

MARKUS WIRTH:

Bernhard's question was not so much what can the chairman do in dealing with the situation but what you do as the other party-appointed arbitrator. How do you react if your counterpart just leans too much to one side and the chair takes a passive attitude?

BERNHARD MEYER:

Correct. It is quite easy to identify a biased arbitrator during a proceeding, but the harder thing is to determine how you, as co-arbitrator, should deal with the situation? If you are abiding by the rules and your counterpart is not, you have a problem. I am interested to know what you do it in such cases?

PIERRE MAYER:

The goal for the co-arbitrators who have different views is to convince the chairman so as to form of majority. If I am not biased but the other one is partial, what proves it is that he says something which is wrong: wrong reasoning, wrong interpretation of the law, et cetera. The only thing I can do is to combat his arguments and try to convince the chairman, not saying directly that the other party is biased because that is impolite and maybe not efficient, but rationally to convince him that the truth is on the other side.

Here of course it is very important to have a good chairman and particularly not a weak chairman. A weak chairman tends to lean in the direction of the one who shouts more loudly. I have had very unpleasant experiences because I was not shouting loud enough although I was right, but that is in maybe one or two cases in my whole life.

MARKUS WIRTH:

That is somewhat contradictory to my own experience. My experience is that very often, if one of the co-arbitrators leans too strongly towards the side of the party that has appointed him there is a natural counter-reaction by the chairman. It may be expressed very actively or in a subtle way but you often see that the chairman starts distancing himself from the arbitrator who too aggressively takes the position of the party that appointed him. If that happens, as a co-arbitrator you can simply lean back and watch the other co-arbitrator driving into the wall because the natural sequence of events then is that the more aggressive one co-arbitrator acts, the more influential the other arbitrator becomes in co-operating with the chairman.

BERNHARD MEYER:

I would agree with this. My own tendency also would be to play the situation down and not to take extreme positions myself. Sometimes, if some procedural requests come up and I find they go too far, I would, however take an opposite position to counter-balance the request. I would try to do this not too loudly because I would rely on the reasonableness of the chairperson. If he/she is sound, the chair will have a natural resistance against the biased arbitrator's requests and my counter request should simply help him/her to turn the request of the biased arbitrator down.

I have another situation which I experienced when I was chairman of an arbitral tribunal and one of my co-arbitrators was very aggressive against some of the witnesses at the hearing. He was selectively aggressive, only against the witnesses of the party that did not appoint him. The co-arbitrator was tougher on those witnesses than opposing counsel. This created a problem because the bias became visible to the outside world. I tried several times to calm the co-arbitrator down and reminded him that he was an arbitrator who should refrain from acting like a counsel. It did not help much. This was a very unpleasant and delicate situation, difficult to manage. You do not want to show to the parties that there are disagreements within the panel.

PHILLIP CAPPER:

Was that an institutional rules arbitration?

BERNHARD MEYER:

It was an institution behind it, yes.

PHILLIP CAPPER:

Did you feel that you should say anything to the institution about your experience?

BERNHARD MEYER:

I was considering it, but I did not do so in this particular case. I did, however, have a hard time with this arbitrator. It went so far that he threatened to file a complaint against me with the Zurich Bar Association, alleging that I would take too much influence on the proceeding and that I would have had private talks with the other arbitrator behind his back. This created a very unpleasant atmosphere, not good for the deliberation process. A hostile atmosphere within the Arbitral Tribunal is really the last thing that I can wish to any arbitrator.

MARKUS WIRTH:

It certainly makes a bad impression on the parties if one of the co-arbitrators is so aggressive towards the witnesses of the "other side" in the witness hearing that the chairman has to intervene and admonish him to change his attitude. This discloses differences within the arbitral tribunal that may damage the integrity of the process.

But dealing with a biased aggressive arbitrator publicly in a hearing is one thing. I think the focus here is how do you deal with him or her in the deliberations? Sometimes it is difficult to distinguish between bias and just stubbornness. I call the latter category of arbitrators, particularly co-arbitrators, the "will not listen" arbitrators; they simply do not listen and routinely repeat their view. How do you deal with that? You have to come to a conclusion but you cannot just cut him or her off — so how do you handle that?

PIERRE MAYER:

I can cite what a certain co-arbitrator said when he was confronted with that situation. There had been aggressive questions by one co-arbitrator. The other co-arbitrator, Professor Fadlallah, turned to the chairman and said "Mr Chairman, would you allow me to cross-examine the witness in turn?" and then he did it but so cleverly that it was a cross-examination but did not look like it. I think that this was a very clever attitude.

MARKUS WIRTH:

We have dealt with bias but we did not deal so much with obstructionist behaviour. What about the situation — I do not know if many of us have experienced it — involving what I call the "leaking arbitrator", namely an arbitrator who discloses certain results of the deliberation to the parties. Normally this shows if one party sometime after the deliberation suddenly comes up with an unsolicited submission that exactly addresses points that were discussed during the deliberation. How do you deal with that situation?

Maybe we can turn to the audience for any comments relating to these issues or other issues that you would like to address.

MARC BLESSING:

We are talking about "pathological situations", and I will share some of my personal experiences; yet, in the end I will conclude that there is no such thing as "pathology in arbitration", but only chances to devise new/appropriate and innovative solutions. And we will be challenged to think "out of the box". I will now describe three scenarios.

First type of "pathological" scenarios: Twenty or thirty years ago we were, specifically in Switzerland, confronted with East/West arbitration in respect of which the Eastern European countries and their State-controlled entities always used the same names/persons as their arbitrators. Hence, some of their nationals (lawyers/professors) got many dozens of nominations, and their independence and ability to act impartially was obviously a matter of serious concern and doubt.

I also had several cases where probably all what was discussed in confidential deliberations of the arbitrators was reported to the party by one of the arbitrators, even during short coffee breaks during the deliberations. And I particularly recall a case — some ten years ago — where I was chair, and Jan Paulsson and an Eastern European Professor serving as the co-arbitrators; during our deliberation sessions in Paris, Jan Paulsson noticed that his colleague and co-arbitrator on the panel used deliberation notes written on stationary of the respective Eastern European party (including a memo and other docs and calculations which were actually prepared by the party, and had not been filed during the arbitral proceedings). Should we (Jan and I) have drawn consequences? No, of course not! We still respected that Eastern European arbitrator as a very long-standing colleague and friend, at the same time realizing that the life as an arbitrator, in some parts of the world, is not exactly as it is meant to be in scholarly writings. However, this kind of situation, I think, we see much less in our days.

A second type of scenarios, which we also see less today, is the party-nominated arbitrator who will tell the chair and his colleague: "I, personally, fully agree with your assessments and resulting decisions, but please understand that, in any event, I will have to write up a dissenting opinion, or otherwise make dissenting views known in the body of the arbitral award, because ..." (among the reasons I heard were, for example: "I have my family in the country ... I have two children who would like to be admitted to the university in my city ...").

These are some of the human realities of life which deserve attention, and we must not speak negatively about such events or arbitrators, but try to approach these situations with understanding, without however compromising the integrity of the process and the correctness of the decision.

Third, I would like to share one of the "worst" (or perhaps most interesting!) "stories" I had: It was a dispute between a US oil company as a claimant, and an Arabic (Gulf State-owned) company as the respondent. The total monetary value of the dispute was in a magnitude of several billions of US dollars (as the value of the particular concession agreement), but before us was only a partial claim of about US$ 380 million for gas deliveries by the US oil company (50% of the gas production of the off-shore gas-field had to be sold to the local utility).

Seat of the tribunal: in a city of the particular Gulf state; applicable law: the local law of that Gulf State "and general principles of law".

The respondent did not name its arbitrator, and so the ICC named a very prestigious and well-known Arabic lawyer (from a different state) as the arbitrator for the (defaulting) Gulf State-respondent.

Already the start of the proceedings was not without surprise: Four weeks before the first hearing, the Arabic arbitrator called me by telephone to say, in short: "Marc, I never travel on public aircrafts. Please organize a private jet for me … otherwise I will not be able to attend the hearing". I then recommended to him to address this kind of request to the ICC counsel in charge, but added that the ICC might not be very sympathetic to entertain such a request.

We then had the Terms of Reference meeting and first hearing in the Gulf State. The respondent party (a Gulf State) did not appear. The Arabic arbitrator, however, did not come alone, but with a whole "entourage" of advisors (university professors from Cairo and Beyrouth, and with Fatih Kemisha as his personal secretary and assistant – Fatih is very well known to many ASA members). In fact, the Arabic arbitrator made it very clear that he would not participate in the hearing without the presence of his personal advisors, and during the meeting/hearing, before contributing to the discussion, he repeatedly took personal advice from his "entourage".

Myself, and my American Co-Arbitrator, were of course a bit surprised, but we did "let it go" and accepted the presence of the "entourage" over and against the protest of the US party (although we felt that this is a bit unusual). But this is only the beginning …

What then happened came as a real shock: On the first day of the hearing, I got served a note by a messenger from the Secretary of the Council of Ministers of the Gulf State (on whose territory we held our hearing) which read, almost literally as I recall, as follows: "I am directed to tell you that the Council of Ministers decided that there shall be no arbitration on this matter."

"There shall be no arbitration in this matter ...!" This was quite a blow! I was given to understand that the natural resources of the particular Gulf State are considered non-arbitrable by the Ruler of the State and its Council of Ministers. Confronted with such an intervention "von hoher Hand", we had to deliberate whether, nevertheless, we could or should continue, and whether—at all—it was at all safe to continue, sitting on the territory of the particular State.

Upon deliberation on the spot, we decided not to accept such a prohibition by the Council of Ministers, and we continued with the hearing. I was then warned to be a *persona non grata* in the particular Gulf State.

In the proceedings, the responding Gulf State did not further participate. This prompted the Arabic co-arbitrator to say "I will now wear two hats. I will be the advocate for the (not-appearing/defaulting) respondent party, and I will at the same time be the arbitrator".

In the further proceedings, our Arabic colleague on the Panel then argued the case as if he was the lawyer, and argued defenses which the Gulf State could possibly invoke in disputing the claim. Whether he in fact also got briefing notes from the respondent State, is a matter which could not be explored; but of course, we (i.e. my American co-arbitrator and myself) could not exclude such a possibility.

How was it for me to deal with such a (unusual) situation? Again, I felt that it would be totally wrong to criticize the position of our Arabic colleague; certainly, it was "quite unusual", to say the least, but—from his Arabic perspective—perfectly legitimate, and within his own perception of the task of serving as a good arbitrator. And, hence, in our private deliberations, he started to privately share arguments which could be invoked against the claim, and which of course were not even heard by the US claimant.

This, however, would have affected the integrity of the process, and something had to be done. But what? My solution was very simple:

I decided to rescue the imbalance between the parties by totally opening up the deliberation phase. We did not have any private deliberations *in camera*, but we had an open floor deliberation among all three arbitrators in front of the claimant, based on a Questionnaire which I had circulated beforehand with numerous issues/aspects which were up for our decision. Of course, the respondent was kept invited to participate, but did not. Also for reaching the final decisions, I circulated a detailed questionnaire of numerous issues which we had to determine and decide on. The Questionnaire was openly circulated to the claimant and to the respondent, so they knew what was going to happen. But, interestingly, while our Arabic arbitrator had taken the advocate's hat for the defaulting respondent, he thereafter was perfectly able to then again wear an arbitrator's hat, when "sitting back" and discussing the final decisions we had to make.

All of this: yes, it is very unusual, to say the least. But: is it wrong?

A scholar with "university bag and baggage" would say: Yes, this is totally wrong and inacceptable, a disaster ... such an arbitrator should have been removed ...! But I would say: Not at all ... we just need to adapt the process ... and convert the "disaster" into an even better process.

We then rendered the award. But how? How did we overcome the prohibition by the Council of Ministers that "there shall be no arbitration", i.e. that the arbitration clause as such was invalid?

Well, we examined — and very carefully interpreted — the applicable law clause in the underlying Concession and Gas Delivery Agreement: that clause provided that the "contract shall be governed by the laws of the [Gulf State] and general principles of law". We were eager to learn everything how this provision came into the Concession and Gas Delivery Contract; and we were keen to learn how this clause was discussed, negotiated, over the several stages of drafts (this is the task of a civil lawyer, but is of course a task a US arbitrator applying common law principles would certainly not undertake).

The essential question was: what should be the relationship between these two references? No really clear answer could be derived from the materials and the contract-negotiation-history. In a 160-page award, we then interpreted the dual reference to mean that, basically, the local Arabic State law must be applied, unless it would stand in stark contradiction to deeply-routed notions pertaining to international law/ general principles of law. Hence, we ascribed to the reference a certain corrective function, in case local law provisions would appear to be incompatible with notions, such as *pacta sunt servanda*, principles of acting in good faith etc. (of course, this description here is a shortcut of what was very carefully argued in the 160-page Arbitral Award). In sum, the reference to general principles, in this context, were seen as a safeguard or safety net, protecting legitimate interests of the parties, in case the local Arabic law would reach a result clearly incompatible with such general principles, notions of good faith etc.

And indeed, under notions of general principles of laws, it would not be permissible, or would indeed be inconceivable, that the head of State or the Council of Ministers could prevent the arbitral proceedings from having their proper course, thereby frustrating the confidence of the other (here: American) party in having the dispute properly determined by way of international arbitration. Hence, we proceeded with the arbitration discarding the Council of Ministers' intervention and prohibition.

But what happened next?

First, I understand that, somehow, our Award was publicized in the United States. And second, about one year later, the particular Gulf State amended its national code (Code of Obligations) and inserted a new provision (according to my memory, a new Article 32) which required two things: First, that in commercial contracts the choice of law provision therein must provide for the applicability of domestic law (of the particular Gulf State), without reference to a foreign law, and second, that any arbitration must take place on the territory of the particular Gulf State (and if the seat of such an arbitral tribunal would be outside, a special governmental approval would be required).

Obviously, this was quite a "dramatic" change of law, which immediately caused very significant concern to future business partners or suppliers engaging in business with parties of that particular Gulf State, or with governmental entities. Consequently, the business community, suppliers of technology etc. reacted in their usual way: They increased the purchase price for deliveries quite significantly so as to take into account doubts (as they existed at that time) regarding the reliability and integrity of arbitration in that Gulf State, independence of arbitrators and "suitability/acceptability" of the local law to govern their relationships.

For sure, this reaction of the business community was becoming a most critical handicap for the further development of the particular Gulf State, and a few years later, that new provision in the Code was again abolished. Since then, the particular Gulf State has seen a truly unprecedented boom, and hosts an international arbitration centre which, today, already has earned very high esteem and respect. Times are changing more rapidly than ever!

I need to add a general post-script to all of my comments:

We have seen, and still see today, situations which appear to be "totally wrong", inacceptable by any standards, unethical, or "pathological". But, in reality: do they disturb? Do they impair the integrity of the arbitral process? Are they, therefore, to be condemned as a serious evil? Or, for instance, is a partisan-arbitrator a "disaster", and should immediately be removed?

My definite answer to such and similar questions is: No!

Such situations in no way impair the integrity of the process, if adequate solutions are devised. Such situations simply must cause us to re-think some aspects, to re-frame the process, and—most of all—to convert different approaches into a better understanding and into an even better process.

Hence, to conclude: there is no such thing as a "pathological" arbitration or procedure, or wrong behavior. So: let's put this term to grave, and let's do more thinking "out of the box".

MARKUS WIRTH:

Thank you for that interesting contribution.

CHRISTOPH LIEBSCHER:

I would like to go back to one issue, which is the hired gun as co-arbitrator and the arguments we have heard on the panel why this is not efficient or sometimes why it may work. It is repeating a bit what you said, Markus, but maybe it is due to the fact that you are a very good chairman and as in real life also with respect to chairs I would argue they follow the bell-shaped distribution. There are a few good ones in the middle, there is luckily a big range of good to moderately good ones, and there are a substantial number of weak chairmen around.

There are two elements that play a role. One is of course the legal training. If you have a legal issue under the jurisdiction of the state the chair was not trained in it and the other co-arbitrator was not trained in either but the hired gun is a professor in that law, it tilts the balance naturally.

The other element I would like to mention is indeed relationship. If you have a co-arbitrator strongly arguing for a party who knows them for 45 years, and you have a newcomer on the other end, it takes lots of experience on the side of the chair to keep the balance in that situation and that is not so infrequent.

On the whole issue of the co-arbitrator's role, I am asking a question which you may say is naive. I have never seen it done but I think "why not?". Why not address in the beginning of the arbitration what the co-arbitrators think their role is and bring it out in the open? Of course people may lie but experience shows that if you look someone in the eye and say "This is how I will do it.", they have a much greater hurdle to pass doing it differently than if this never happens. In my experience it works.

What I do in the so-called Procedural Order No 1, it may be considered redundant but it is based on past experience, is to put usually a provision about communication in the sense that communication is to the arbitral tribunal as a rule and nobody else. Maybe it works, maybe it does not, I do not know, but I think it is better spelling these things out than not doing it.

WILLIAM BASSLER:

I just want to comment on Dr Wirth's observation which I recently experienced, the distinction between stubbornness and bias, a situation in which one of the issues was an issue of law. There were published opinions on it. It seemed self-evident to me and the other co-arbitrator but the third arbitrator, who assured us he had read the cases, thought we were wrong. I was absolutely perplexed by this person's position. It brought into position something else said earlier in the discussions about bargaining. As I was trying to figure out what to do—I was not the chair, we had a weak chair unfortunately—this stubborn arbitrator wanted to add something to the opinion which I thought was off the mark and superfluous but benign. At the appropriate moment I indicated I could go along with his benign suggestion providing that he revisited his position on what I called the invincible ignorance and it worked to my surprise, so you never know.

MARKUS WIRTH:

That is a perfect bridge to our next sub-topic. I am sorry we cannot hear everybody from the audience who wished to comment— we are quite advanced in time and should proceed. The second sub-topic, namely bargaining, is what was just touched upon by Mr Bassler. Bernhard Meyer will further explore that topic.

Structuring a Bargaining Process

Bernhard F. Meyer

BERNHARD MEYER:

To warm up the discussion if and how a bargaining process should be structured, I would like to present a recent, very illustrative case. I will be very specific when opening the black box, and I will open it quite a bit. The case was an ICC arbitration proceeding. The language was English, but everything else was Greek. The parties were Greek companies (although one was foreign controlled). Both co-arbitrators were Greek law professors. The applicable law was Greek law. Only the Chairman, I, was from Switzerland. The hearings were fixed by the parties to take place in Athens, although the formal seat of the arbitration was in Zurich.

Considering the backgrounds of the parties, the panel members and most of the witnesses, I felt pretty lonely. I was the only person in the whole proceeding that was not a Greek national, and I did not speak Greek. I had the additional handicap that I was unable to read the applicable legal acts and court decisions in their original form, as they were written in the Cyrillic alphabet. I had translations of some texts, but they were unofficial and of doubtful quality.

The case turned on the early termination of a very substantial supply contract for pharmaceutical products. Under the contract, the respondent ordered and committed to take delivery of a large amount of special pharmaceuticals over a certain period of time. The pharmaceuticals were manufactured in accordance with an agreed delivery schedule.

Halfway down the contract period, respondent terminated the contract, alleging a substantial change of the circumstances and "good cause" for the termination. Claimant challenged the termination, insisting on specific performance or payment of damages in lieu of performance.

The principle sounds easy, but the case was full of legal and procedural pitfalls. There were a series of ancillary questions that needed to be addressed in this case. For instance, respondent alleged an inadmissible transformation of a compensation claim (in the request for arbitration), into a performance claim (in the full statement of claim). Then, claimant alleged that an early termination was only possible for a standing contract under Greek law (a so called "continuous contract") but not for a non-standing contract ("fixed-term"). Thus, the qualification of the contract under Greek law was important. If the contract was a standing contract, then the additional legal question was to be addressed if the grounds for termination were proven. Thus, the arbitral tribunal had to resolve many preliminary and procedural issues before addressing the material claims.

The lawyers who were arguing the case were predominantly Greek law professors, and my two co-arbitrators were Greek law professors as well. I indeed learned a lot about Greek law in this case. However, what is more important from the perspective that we are discussing today is the fact that the two co-arbitrators thoroughly supported the respective positions of the parties that had appointed them. It was clear at a very early stage of the proceeding that it was my role and duty to make the final decision.

My situation, thus, was as follows: I knew that the internal discussions and the bargaining with my two learned Greek co-arbitrators would be intense. I had to make the final decisions, although my knowledge of and accessibility to Greek law and Greek legal sources was very limited. It was also clear under the circumstances that I had to write the final award. Although my two co-arbitrators were Greek law professors, they would have written two totally different awards under the circumstances.

How did I cope with this situation?

You will find the answer in your file, at tab 14 [see p. 135 below]. I created a tool for structuring our internal discussions, namely a very detailed decision tree. The decision tree was drafted along the specific issues of this case. You may not understand every detail of this tree, but what was essential for my purposes was the fact that I listed all issues in a logical manner, including the various potential decisions, but without indicating my preference. For instance, there was one line of issues to be addressed if the termination was valid. If the termination was invalid, the line of issues would be a different one. I then I submitted this decision tree, more or less in the form you have here, to my co-arbitrators and I asked them, as a first step, to only agree to the logic inherent in the decision tree. I did not ask for any opinions at this stage, I just wanted my co-arbitrators to agree to the main issues and the logical follow-up of the issues mentioned therein.

After some small changes, we agreed that the decision tree and the logic behind it were correct. Then, we entered into phase two: I asked both co-arbitrators to write down for me, in the form of very short opinions, how they would decide the listed issues. The assignment was to address all issues that were listed in the decision tree, and not only the ones they personally considered to be relevant.

For instance, if one co-arbitrator took the position that the contract termination was valid, he still was required to address the issues that did come up under the hypothesis that the Arbitral Tribunal did not sustain the termination. In doing so, I asked the co-arbitrators to also cite the legal provisions and the legal authorities that support their respective opinions on the treated issues. The idea, back in my mind, was that once I had to write the final award, I had one or even two specific opinions to draw from in response to the decision tree (including references to the supporting law and judicial literature). In addition, this gave me the opportunity to lead the discussion between the arbitrators during the subsequent deliberations.

The two law professors, who were good friends in their personal lives, but far apart in their views about this case, went perfectly along with this procedure. They both wrote relatively short memorandums on all issues listed in the decision tree, outlining their thinking and the legal sources supporting their opinions.

Only once I was in possession of these two memorandums, did I organise the first deliberation meeting in Zurich. By that time, I had a good understanding of what my co-arbitrators' positions were on all issues, and I understood what their preferred outcome would be. As expected, each co-arbitrator clearly favoured the case advanced by the party appointing them.

At the deliberations, I wanted to talk about the facts only. On that level, I was able to manage the discussion perfectly. Facts remain facts, whether they are considered under Greek, German or Swiss law. The plan was that we had to agree to a proven fact scenario and that all legal issues would then fall into place thereafter.

I purposely did not address the facts surrounding the termination first, although this was the most critical issue. Rather, we started "backwards", with less critical parts of the decision tree. We had good debates about the various options. When doing this, it became quite obvious that the factual assumptions on which my Co-Arbitrators relied were very different, along the lines that were argued by the two parties. I had my own understanding of the facts and tried to convince my co-arbitrators thereof. The good thing in this process was that once I made an independent decision as to the facts underlying a given issue, the two co-arbitrators, most of the time, were able to agree with each other as to the legal consequences thereof. So, once an agreement on the relevant facts was reached amongst the three of us, or was decided by me in my capacity as neutral chair (if there was no agreement between the co-arbitrators), the legal conclusions therefrom were no longer in debate. By focusing on the facts rather than on legal consequences, most of the issues listed in the decision tree could be resolved in a manner satisfactory to all three of us.

One of the issues that we had to address in the course of this backwards deliberation process was the size of the damage to be granted to the claimant in case the early termination by respondent should not be upheld by the arbitral tribunal (an issue that was still open at that time). There, it became quite clear that one co-arbitrator, the one appointed by the party declaring the termination, would be flexible on the termination issue if the damage amount resulting from an invalid termination would not be excessively high. The other co-arbitrator, who was appointed by the party alleging invalidity of the early termination, was willing to compromise on the damage amount under such scenario. But respondent's position that no damage did in fact occur, even if the contract termination should be considered as invalid, was hotly debated. The outcome was that a reasonable solution would be possible. So, while on the face of it, my co-arbitrators still maintained their strong positions on the termination and on the damage issues, it was quite evident by that time that there was flexibility on both sides to compromise.

When we got to the termination issue, I had a clear opinion: I felt that the (high) threshold for a substantial change of circumstances, or of a termination for good cause, was not reached in this case and that the principle "*pacta sunt servanda*" should prevail. I was also of the opinion that the damage calculated by the claimant under the hypothesis of an invalid termination was grossly exaggerated. At least some of the damage was (or could have been) avoided simply by stopping the production process once it became clear that respondent would no longer fulfil the contract. So, apart from other shortcomings, the claimant failed to mitigate the damage. Based on our prior discussion, I proposed a solution which I believed to be right, fair and acceptable to both co-arbitrators. I noticed from our previous discussions that if the damage assessment was reasonable, then the arbitrator, who was originally taking the position that the termination was to be upheld, would also agree to the contrary solution, provided the assessed damage was reasonable. So, my proposal was that the termination should be declared invalid, but that the claimed damage should be reduced substantially, due to the previously discussed shortcomings. After some discussion (one might call this a bargaining process), my solution was acceptable to both co-arbitrators. The end result was a unanimous decision.

Based on the previously submitted memos of the two co-arbitrators, I was also able to write the first draft of the award, even though it was under Greek law. My co-arbitrators further redacted the award and brought it to its final form. The whole process was very smooth in the end, although it looked very difficult in the beginning.

What I would like to say about this case is the following: At the beginning and in the end, there was indeed a bargaining process between the arbitrators. But it was primarily fact driven. Yes, we did bargain, and we did make "deals" as described. But, I do not think that the result was, what Professor Bernardini called this morning, a *compromise*. I think the end result was a balanced decision where the majority of the arbitral tribunal came to the conclusion that the facts of the case did not support a premature termination. On the other hand, the damage claimed needed to be substantially lowered, due to the shortcomings in claimant's reaction once it was clear that the (invalid) termination was irreversible.

The bargaining process allowed the Arbitral Tribunal to examine all relevant issues in great depth and to arrive at a balanced, finally unanimous, award.

Is such process good or bad? I think we can have an interesting debate about this afterwards. What is clear for me is that we would have ended up with three different awards in this case had we not taken the described approach. We would have had a decision by one co-arbitrator appointed by the claimant, and a totally different one by the co-arbitrator appointed by respondent. My chairman's opinion would again have been fundamentally different from the two since I did not agree with one co-arbitrator on the termination issue, but I did, likewise, not agree with the other co-arbitrator on the damage assessment. Under the ICC Rules, my chairman's decision would have become the final award, but it would have been weakened by assumingly two dissenting opinions (one on the termination and one on the damage issues). Would that have been better than a "bargained" result? I do not think so. The process which I describe here ended in exactly the same result, namely the one which the Chairman proposed. But, it was — as a result of the bargaining process — a unanimous decision, signed by all three arbitrators, to everyone's satisfaction.

I personally think that a bargaining process, as long as it is based on facts and leads to a result acceptable to all members of the Arbitral Tribunal, is the best way to deal with a situation where the opinions of the arbitrators go far apart. The negotiation process leads to a better and more convincing result than a decision with one or even two dissenting opinions, leaving the parties at a loss of what the correct outcome of the case should be.

MARKUS WIRTH:

That is an interesting thesis. My question is: does it really produce a good decision if you have a hotly disputed decision on liability where you have a clear two-to-one situation, and then in order to mitigate the effect of the harsh majority decision on liability all the arbitrators in turn agree to exercise reluctance in respect of the quantum? I would be interested to have the views of the audience, first of all, whether people have, as arbitrators, experienced that situation and, secondly, whether from a party perspective they appreciate this kind of trying to find a compromise.

CHRISTOPH LIEBSCHER:

As an arbitrator and party counsel I am not in favour of mitigating. This whole bargaining thing of course is fully understandable where there is a preliminary element, such as liability, that is clear. If there is not, of course it is good practice to really make sure that everybody understands what everybody is thinking and saying. After that to me that box would be closed and then we start from scratch for the next issue.

I have even seen as a chairman, I admit, some mitigating effects in quantum but they were *de minimis*; they were minor issues given the total amount of the claim. Indeed I, in the end, agreed to go along with a mitigated solution rather than waste unnecessary time and effort on something that materially does not matter.

CHRISTOPHER KOCH:

From a parties' perspective, if you can have a majority award for a million you have got to be happier than if you get a unanimous award for 500,000. From the president's perspective, I think there is a tendency to want to have a unanimous decision because I think one has the feeling that it reflects more the equities of the case. I think what you get into is the splitting of the baby syndrome there.

I had the experience in Paris recently where an arbitrator basically threatened a dissenting opinion and for me I felt that would be a failure on my part if I let that dissenting opinion go so we tried to get him back on board. We managed to do it with exactly the same result but compromising on some of the reasoning.

MARKUS WIRTH:

In that connection I would like to refer you to a PowerPoint slide that is included in the conference material under tab 11. It is an excerpt from the last statistical report of the ICC. They report that during the year 2011 a total of 285 partial and final awards were rendered by three member tribunals and in these cases 244 awards, or 85.6%, were rendered unanimously, and 41, meaning 14.4%, by a majority of the arbitrators comprising the tribunal.

Somehow that strikes me as odd. I have difficulty believing that in 86% of all the cases all three arbitrators were of the same opinion - unless they arrived at their unanimous decision by some kind of bargaining.

The question that I would like to put to the audience: is our goal, particularly from the perspective of a chairman, to strive for a unanimous decision or is it to reach the correct decision even if it involves dissenting opinions?

I confess I do not have any problem with dissenting opinions in arbitrations I am chairing. We will hear more about the forms dissenting opinions may take but I think it does not undermine an award if within the body of the award it is noted where there is a majority decision and the minority view is briefly summarised. It does not undermine the award; it simply shows that the arbitrators have deliberated diligently, that views have clashed and that finally the case was decided according to what the majority thought would be right.

HANSJOERG STUTZER:

Please allow me to come back quickly to the issue of bias. I always understood that the prerequisite strict pre-condition for being an arbitrator is to be strictly independent. I do not understand how you can sit as an arbitrator independent and be biased. I am asking if while sitting at an arbitrator panel seeing a co-arbitrator being biased, meaning obviously not independent, you do not have a duty to correct that?

PHILLIP CAPPER:

One has a duty to deal with it. Correction may be impossible: avoidance of its impact is essential if it can be achieved. At that point I think it becomes a very pragmatic question of the kinds of techniques we discussed whether by the co-arbitrator or the chair. Ultimately one wants the right and proper result to be recorded in an enforceable award. To some extent it may lead to this present topic, the dissenting opinion, which may be a practical way of dealing with it.

PAOLO MICHELE PATOCCHI:

The first comment is about possible definitions of negotiation or concession or bargaining among arbitrators. It would seem to me that the process whereby one arbitrator seeks to persuade another that his views are not entirely correct is really an absolutely normal part in each and every deliberation. I would, for my part, not characterise that as any form of bargaining. I would suggest that it is more helpful to define bargaining or concession in a far narrower way by referring to situations in which one arbitrator is amenable to concurring with another provided that a point is conceded and there is a kind of *quid pro quo* that takes place in the deliberation. That is a point of definition and it was my first comment.

The second comment is about the requirements that would have to be met in order for that kind of discussion or bargaining to take place. Professor Bernardini earlier this morning referred to cases in which the answer to an issue is unclear and all arbitrators appear to agree that it is not easy to give one answer to such issue, and more than one answer may be correct to some extent and there is therefore a particular difficulty to be solved. It would seem to me that there are other cases, for instance the threat of the dissent which might endanger the enforceability of the award because one is dealing with enforcement in a jurisdiction which is not particularly arbitration friendly, and it would seem to me that it might be helpful to seek views from the audience as to the kind of particular situations that have to be considered.

At the risk of making many enemies in this room I would like to make one last comment on bias. We have heard concrete examples of bias referring to a number of undesignated countries in Eastern Europe and Greece was mentioned, and I will not name any other. I would like to agree with Professor Mayer when he says that he has seen bias quite often in his practice and it has been my experience as well. I would readily accept that bias exists in this country as well and we should not hide that. This is a difficulty one has in each and every jurisdiction depending on the colleagues one is sitting with.

MARKUS WIRTH:

You raised a few interesting issues and questions and we may perhaps best discuss those over lunch. Time is advancing and I would like to now turn in more detail to our third sub-topic, the dissenting opinion.

Dealing with Dissenting Opinions

Pierre Mayer

PIERRE MAYER:

The subject has already been partially dealt with this morning so I will make my comments briefer. Dissenting opinions raise, on the one hand, legal and practical issues, and I will address them, but essentially they invite us to ask ourselves as arbitrators, co-arbitrators most often, is it legitimate to write a dissenting opinion? Is it even sometimes necessary and, maybe depending on the circumstances, is it advisable or permissible from an ethical point of view to write a dissenting opinion or to insist that it be mentioned in the award?

From a legal and practical perspective, first I think one must distinguish two kinds of dissenting opinions. The first kind consists in a special mention in the award that one arbitrator is dissenting; it can also mention the reasons why he or she is dissenting and also the identity of the dissenting arbitrator, or not mention the identity or not mention the reasons. There are several ways of presenting the existence of a dissent.

I think that raises no serious problem because necessarily that can take place only if a majority of the arbitrators agrees with the mention of this dissent in the award, since it is part of the award. That is accepted I think everywhere and there are English decisions, for instance, to that effect.

One could object, it is true, that such a practice infringes the principle of secrecy of deliberations but what is exactly the meaning of that principle? Obviously until the award is rendered the secret is absolute, at least it should be, but once the award is rendered the situation is quite different. I see no compelling reason to conceal the fact that there was a majority view and there was a minority view. Of course, what remains not to be made public is the detail of the discussions. In that sense there is secrecy. You must not go all over the place saying "I had this argument but the other ones answered this but finally I convinced them." That is secret but as to the existence of the dissent and even the reasons for the dissent I see no problem.

The other kind of dissenting opinion is the opinion expressed in a separate document and I will focus on that situation. Such opinions are not infrequent. I have another statistical source. An ICC survey revealed that in the year 2003—maybe there is more recent information but I do not have it—7% of the awards rendered in 2003 in the ICC context were accompanied by a dissenting opinion in the form of a separate document. Coming to more legal aspects, also practical, from another ICC survey made in 1988 by a working party chaired by Martin Hunter, it appeared that in none of the countries of the survey dissenting opinions were prohibited.

What is the legal and practical status of dissenting opinions? I would say that generally it is the following. First, they are not considered part of the award except in the case of ICSID, and I will come back to this. Second, they have no legal authority, they are just what they are, the opinion of an arbitrator. Third, and that is probably debatable, no-one, not even the majority, can prevent the dissenting arbitrator from communicating his or her dissent to the parties. It would be too easy for the majority to say "You want to criticise us, we say no, you cannot." I think it is a legitimate right to draft and communicate a dissenting opinion to the parties. Is it always advisable, that is another question.

Fourth, in institutional arbitration the dissent is normally transmitted to the institution either with the award or after the majority award has been transmitted, and we heard this morning that in one case the dissent came even before the award was there. Then the dissenting opinion is notified by the institution to the parties together with the award, although it is not a part of the award.

Specifically in ICC arbitration we know that there is a scrutiny of the awards by the Court. The dissent has been transmitted to it. I have read different descriptions but in one of them it is said that while exercising its scrutiny on the award the Court has a look at the dissenting opinion, but it does not make any judgment on the dissenting opinion; it does not approve it or disapprove it. The Court communicates the dissenting opinion to the parties except if it appears that that would jeopardise the possibility of enforcing the award, which does not seem to be very frequent or maybe does not even exist at all.

Now I come to the second aspect: the psychological and ethical aspect. Under what circumstances is it legitimate or even advisable to make a dissenting opinion? There is no unanimity there but I think, and that was already mentioned this morning by Piero Bernardini, that there is a big difference between investment and particularly ICSID arbitration and, on the other hand, commercial arbitration. In ICSID arbitration there is every reason for the dissenting arbitrator, the one who does not agree, to draft a dissenting opinion. There are various reasons, at least one of them was mentioned by Piero Bernardini. The first reason is that the Washington Convention mentions explicitly the possibility, the right, for an arbitrator to "attach his individual opinion to the award." It is somewhat ambiguous: "to attach to the award;" does it mean that it is part of the award, or not part? The answer is given in the Arbitration Rules of ICSID, Article 48: "The Secretary General shall despatch a certified copy of the award including individual opinions and statements of dissent."

The separate or dissenting opinion is part of the award.

The second reason is that there is a very strong polarisation among arbitrators between those who are clearly pro-State and those who are clearly pro-investors. There are some who are neutral, and they are more often appointed chairman, but this polarisation exists and, therefore, when one co-arbitrator is in the minority he wants it to be known that he does not agree with the majority.

Thirdly, the reason was given by Piero Bernardini, these ICSID awards create a case law and so every opinion expressed, even a minority one, is part of the bulk of opinions and is relied upon later on. That is for investment arbitration.

As to commercial arbitration, there is a lot of hostility towards dissenting opinions. There is the argument of secrecy of deliberations, which does not convince me, but there are other more convincing arguments. First, dissenting opinions underscore the link between the arbitrator and the party appointing him or her. The partial arbitrator will make a dissenting opinion just to show his zeal in favour of "his" party, and that is wrong. Also sometimes the goal pursued by the dissenting arbitrator is to weaken the award by pointing to possible grounds for having it set aside and that is also wrong. There are good reasons to dislike dissenting opinions.

At this point it is necessary to distinguish two kinds of dissenting opinions: those, on the one hand, that expose an irregularity in the procedure, and those that criticise the reasoning of the majority. In the first case some authors, for instance Redfern and Hunter, consider that it is even the duty to expose any serious wrongdoing which might have affected the result and I tend to agree.

In the second case, the dissent would only expose an intellectual disagreement with the majority. I think there is in the mind of the arbitrator a struggle between opposite considerations. On the one side there is a legitimate desire to express what he thinks is the correct solution or reasoning and to distance himself from the errors made by the majority, which is a legitimate ambition. On the other side, there should be a mixture of modesty and fair play. There was a discussion, a debate, and the arbitrator was in a minority. There is an award, a majority award, and the minority should admit defeat.

Another consideration in the same direction is that the dissenting arbitrator does not want to be suspected of being partial, at least some people have that pre-occupation, but the problem is, and I think that is the central point, that the intellectually dissenting arbitrator fears that the party that has appointed him or her will conclude, if the award is rendered without any mention that it is a majority award, or without any dissenting opinion, and is signed by the three arbitrators, that he agrees with the other arbitrators when in fact he disagrees, he sincerely disagrees. I think it should be understood, and that is crucial, by counsel and parties, and counsel should explain to the parties, that not writing a dissenting opinion does not mean that one shares the position expressed in the award.

The normal solution, whether you agree or not, is to sign and not make a dissenting opinion except, and in fact that is the answer if I may propose one, that all depends on the seriousness of the disagreement. I would think that it is only in cases where the majority view is, in the mind of the other arbitrator, not only erroneous but really shocking that the dissenting opinion is legitimate. In other cases, you should accept that you have been defeated. That is my personal view.

MARKUS WIRTH:

Do we have any reaction from the audience to this last position taken by Pierre?

ANDREAS REINER:

I have no problem with dissenting opinions. Number one, it takes off pressure from the deliberation and I agree with what Markus Wirth said. If you realize from the beginning or in the deliberation that some co-arbitrator might try to exercise that pressure hoping that the chair or the other will give in in order to reach a unanimous decision, I am puzzled by the idea of bargaining. That is not doing justice. If you and one other member of the tribunal believe that X is right, why would you bargain just to a get a unanimous decision? I am not sure what the legitimacy is for that approach.

There are, of course, situations where there are factual reasons why things are neither white nor black. If that is what you mean by bargaining then it is just a proper analysis of the case. It may simply be a more detailed analysis. There may be mitigating factors. There may be a duty that has been violated to mitigate damages. There may be a shared liability. That is law; that is not bargaining. That is just the proper analysis of the merits of the case.

Why bargain? There is no factual reason for doing it and no legal reason. Where is the legitimacy for doing that? I heard what Michele Patocchi said: it may increase the chances of enforcement but how do you know? Is that a point discussed with the parties? Did you ask the parties' views on that? Would they agree? Do you know where the award is going to be enforced? Assuming you believe that 10 million is the right figure and you say perhaps their chances of enforcement are increased if we just give 5. If some jurisdiction might refuse enforcement because of a dissenting opinion, those jurisdictions might find other reasons for not enforcing the decision. Then the party which would have been justified legally to 10 million might end up having to bargain down again from the 5 million to 4, or even less. I do not find that justified.

One point as to disclosing the reasons for dissent: what I both as a chairman or as party counsel find quite frustrating is to read that somebody dissented without knowing why. There are two options. It does happen that the minority is right and the majority is wrong. I think it is a good thing for the parties to know that there was a debate and perhaps the minority was right but that is part of the game. It is the majority that decides and there is no absolute guarantee that the majority is right. Why not be transparent and open in that respect?

If you just say "dissenting" without saying why, that I find unhelpful because you might have lots of suspicions of why one was dissenting. Perhaps the arbitrator was lazy, that is the easiest explanation. You might suspect the process was not OK, which would not be a very good explanation either. I think it helps the process if it is transparent: the arbitrators disagreed on certain points and each party must make their own judgment of it.

BRUCE GAILEY:

Markus Wirth identified tension between unanimity and reaching the correct decision. I am glad that some of my colleagues have raised a third tension which is enforceability. As a user that is a subject very dear to my heart. I have seen what I think has been horse trading on points of principle on legal issues in order to obtain what I think is a unanimous decision and that in itself has led to issues of enforceability.

I will give you one example as people are relating to their war stories. We had a situation in which one party terminated for cause the contract. Normally I tell our people internally when you terminate for cause, someone is in breach. Either you are entitled to terminate because the other party is in breach or you got it wrong and the other party is not in breach and your termination is in breach, that is normal.

We had a case in which I think there was a horse trade and the result was no-one was in breach. There was still an award in favour of one party but that result potentially leads to difficulty in enforcement when the courts locally say "How can that be? That is against public policy for us to enforce an award which is so clearly wrong on the law."

I caution those who engage in horse trading that perhaps having a dissenting opinion could result in problems of enforceability. Horse trading on the principles could also result in problems of enforceability.

PIERRE MAYER:

I totally agree with Andreas Reiner on his point that there is no reason except, in very exceptional circumstances, but normally there is no reason, to bargain. What you have to do as an arbitrator is to render a just award and whether it is unanimous or not is not such a problem.

On the other point, I disagree. First, the fact that there is one arbitrator who disagrees with the others is not such a big issue even if there is no dissenting opinion. There are discussions and in the end there is a majority award. It does not necessarily take so much time to try to convince the arbitrator who disagrees; you do not convince him and you render the award. Your position I think has the following drawback. If you say it is normal, if you disagree, to issue a dissenting opinion, then it will be expected by the community that an arbitrator who disagrees must render a dissenting opinion and if he does not that means he agrees. Then dissenting opinions will not be exceptional, 7%, they will be systematic. Everybody, every arbitrator, and we know that they are often somewhat biased, will feel obliged to issue a dissenting opinion and I think that entails a lot of work, first and, second, that is not the best process.

MARKUS WIRTH:

This has been a very interesting discussion. I have a little bit of a problem as we are running 30 minutes late. Looking at the organiser I think we should stop. This is the time to follow instructions! And indeed, I believe the majority, if not unanimous view, is that we are all hungry and deserve lunch!

However, before we break for lunch I would like to thank my co-panellists very much for their spirited contributions and the open statement of their positions. I also would like to thank the contributors from the audience who have added some very refreshing thoughts to our discussion.

Panel 3

Assistance to the Tribunal: Options, Advantages and Dangers

Moderated by Michael E. Schneider

MICHAEL E. SCHNEIDER:

Addressing the participants in the audience still standing, engaged in discussions: Can the dissenting arbitrators please leave the room so that the deliberations are in consensus and no horse trading! Those who do not want to dissent, please sit down.

Welcome to this afternoon's session. Before we start the session there are two points. First, I had from one of our colleagues here an excellent idea. He sat with Daniel Wehrli recently in an arbitration and he suggested to add in the memorial note which we will be publishing in the forthcoming Bulletin a short note commemorating on his experience with Daniel. I am addressing all the many others in the room who sat with him in arbitrations or worked with him: if you would be prepared to add such a note on your memories with Daniel, please send it to me in the next ten days and it would be a very nice tribute to his memory.

The second point is that as I mentioned this morning we record the conference. All your contributions will be published. There are a number of you who have sent them in at the last minute or who think that in the follow-up of this discussion here there are things which you want to contribute. As you have seen this morning we cannot hear all the contributions from the floor, if you think you would like to make comments on certain subjects please feel free to do so and send them to Bernhard Berger. Anything that comes to your mind, not just notes you have, observations you have but also experiences like a dissenting opinion or how an arbitrator was dealing with dissent or other communications. You have in the folder for instance Bernhard Meyer's decision tree, experience like this, send it to Bernhard Berger and we will put it in the book.

The subject for this afternoon is somewhat different. The paradigm we have in arbitration is that the arbitrators are chosen for their personal qualifications. They are expected to read the file. They are expected to attend the hearing and not, as we heard about this one arbitrator, walk out in the middle of the hearing. They are expected to write the decision: procedural decisions and primarily the award. As we know, writing your opinions down, and again we heard this this morning, is part of the thinking process so the drafting of the award is an important aspect of the decision making.

This paradigm probably was created or arose in a time when you had relatively simple cases. You had one party perhaps with a lawyer and another party perhaps also with a lawyer or the parties themselves and sometimes they had difficult questions but the cases were relatively simple even if there are important legal questions at stake. Today we have seen important changes in the way our arbitrations are discussed: to start with, the way the parties' case is presented. It is sufficient to look into some of the hearings we are attending where you have on the claimant's side five, ten, fifteen people sitting in two rows and similar numbers on the respondent's side and you have the submissions. I have one where I have 20 boxes for one Statement of Claim, 20 boxes each with six or eight folders. You have large numbers of lawyers and experts who prepare the case and, on the other side, the Tribunal members are faced with all of what I called on some occasions the paper tsunami: you have one or three or four individuals who have to deal with this mass.

At some stage I recommended that a tribunal should require of lead counsel a written declaration that the lead counsel he or she has read every page they submit to the arbitrators that they expect the arbitrators to read! That is one part of it.

Another part of it is the technical complication of the issues that are brought before us, not just the variety of issues but also the level at which these technical issues are argued with experts' opinions which can be longer than the leading submissions. Sometimes I have seen that at the end of the procedure, when we look at the costs, the costs for the experts are higher than those for the lawyers. In other words, the technicality and the nature and type of technical issues we have to deal with equally are increasing.

Then we have the question of the time of the arbitrator. What does an arbitrator spend his time on usefully? We have arbitrators who have become professional arbitrators who do this for their livelihood and whom you chose because they have judgment. We always see the same faces and the comments: why always these? When you look for a chairman, especially for a chairman, you say this is a man or woman in whom I have trust. They are in demand and if they are not very rigorous with the number of cases they accept then the question is: how do these people spend their time best?

PANEL 3: ASSISTANCE TO THE TRIBUNAL

When considering whether any of this work an arbitrator has to do he or she can delegate, the question is do I want this person for his balanced judgment or do I wish the arbitrator to do all the work? Then the question is that of the value added to the thinking process by writing everything yourself: is that sufficient to justify the longer time of the preparation?

That is the theme and there are different responses to this scenario. One is to say we do not care, that is the paradigm and that is the mandate of the arbitrator, that is his responsibility and if she can handle only three cases a year because they are so complex let her only take three cases, or you can say shall we look into the decision-making process whether there are changes that can be made, that can be adjusted.

What we are trying to do now is not pass judgment on whether one or the other approach is right. We are simply trying to present forms in which arbitrators may obtain assistance in one way or another and simply put this on the table, discuss amongst ourselves and with you what are the implications of one form or another of assistance and what are the risks. What needs to be regulated or should we exclude any assistance at all?

We propose to address the subject in three stages. The first stage is what I would call the landscape: to get an overview of how in different bodies in different circumstances the combination of the arbitrator and those who are assisting can be organised. We will then have a look into the contributions from the assistants, how this actually works in the actual interaction between the arbitrator and the persons who assist. In the third stage we will look at what are the risks and the manners in which to deal with them.

When we go through the landscape we will start with Andrea Meier who will give an overview of a number of different forms that she has come across or we collectively have come across. We will then have three specific examples: one is the subject about which Hans van Houtte has written, the document production master and expert facilitator, a specific type of intervener or person providing a particular service; we will have Zachary Douglas to tell us more about the subject which is probably the one you expect us all to talk about, the secretary; and the third is an example of a particularly intense off-loading of the decision-making process into the support service, the secretariat and the experts which is probably carried furthest in the United Nations Compensation Commission where you have a large secretariat and a large team of experts. Geoffrey Senogles was part of the secretariat and the experts and we will have a discussion whether there are any lessons we can learn from this experience for our work in arbitration.

I will not present to you in detail the panellists as you have their CVs in your folder. I recommend that you look at the CVs because these are all important persons. You will discover new things about the many varied activities they have done so look at them carefully. Also, you will find at the end of the conference folder and in separate tabs interesting material to follow-up on our discussion.

The only thing I would say as presentation is Andrea Meier is president of ASA below 40 and we are grateful for the work she contributes to our Association in this function.

Assistance to the Tribunal: an Overview

Andrea Meier

ANDREA MEIER:

I have to say it is a great honour to be on this panel with such esteemed and also nice colleagues. I am pleased to start off the discussion with an overview of the different forms of assistance that are potentially available to the tribunal.

In my overview I will talk about expert assistance, expert teaming, special masters, less common forms of assistance by the institutions and last but not least the secretary to the tribunal.

It is safe to say that there is general consensus today that a tribunal may appoint its own expert unless all parties object. However, arbitration laws and rules providing for the appointment of a tribunal-appointed expert normally follow a traditional notion of the expert role. That role consists of the expert writing an expert report on which the parties may comment.

There are, however, other ways in which an expert may provide assistance to the tribunal. Because this falls outside of the traditional expert role, I refer to this type of expert as expert assistant. You will find other names used for the same purpose such as expert adviser or, in England, assessor; often though he is simply referred to as expert.

There are a number of tasks for which expert assistance may be retained. Depending on the needs of the case they may be appointed for only one, some or all of these tasks. This makes the expert assistant a very flexible instrument. Given that he is used beyond the traditional role of tribunal-appointed expert, however, it is particularly important that the tribunal consult with the parties on the tasks it intends to assign to him and they are each defined in the expert Terms of Reference.

Courtesy of Michal E. Schneider you will find some examples of a Terms of Reference for an expert assistant in your binder, tab 16 and 20,[1] so I hope you find the time to look at them.

Moving on to the specific task of the expert assistant: one is co-ordinating the parties' experts. It is not uncommon that the parties' experts come to very different results as we have all experienced. There are ways for the tribunal to reduce these differences mainly by inviting the experts to sit together and draft joint lists of issues.

---

[1] *See infra* p. 151.

For co-ordinating purposes the tribunal may wish to obtain an expert assistant as facilitator. Let me direct you to the Terms of Reference for a scheduling expert which you find in the seminar binder at tab 16.[2] If you look at section 1(b), the experts' task is meeting with the parties' respective experts to identify those facts and issues on which they agree and clarify and focus the points on which they disagree. Section 1(c) provides that the expert may be asked to prepare a report in that regard. The expert assistant acting as facilitator will be discussed in more detail by Hans van Houtte.

Another possible task of an expert assistant which is not specifically mentioned in these Terms of Reference is the preparation of working tools for the tribunal such as spread sheets and formula for quantum calculation, for example, for the purpose of calculating damages caused by delay in construction arbitration.

If you look again into our Terms of Reference we can see that a further task is responding to questions of the tribunal. As it says in section 1(d) the expert will "respond to questions the tribunal has with respect to scheduling matters as they arise in the arbitration." Such a provision allows for a flexible co-operation between the tribunal and the expert assistant as the tribunal may turn to the assistant whenever the need arises. However, this flexibility should not be achieved at the price of the parties' right to the heard.

A traditional safeguard on this right can be found in our Terms of Reference. According to section 2:

> Any questions put by the tribunal to the expert and any answer or report produced by the expert shall be made available to the parties who will be provided with an opportunity to comment on the report and make submissions to the tribunal in regard of it.

An expert assistant may also be asked to attend evidentiary hearings in order to participate in the examination of the party-appointed expert. The expert assistant is usually allowed directly to ask questions to the party-appointed expert. Due to his expertise he is in a position to effectively test the opinions of these experts.

It may also occur that tribunals conduct meetings with the expert assistant in the absence of the parties and invite him to attend the tribunal's deliberations. Practitioners in support of this practice point out that it can be useful to have the expert present when discussing the very technical issues to make sure that the tribunal has understood

---

[2] *See infra* p. 151.

them properly. Others categorically dismiss this practice because of the risk of undue influence on the decision-making process. I am sure we will get back to this issue including possible measures of precaution in our later discussion.

Before leaving the topic of the expert assistant let me add a few words on the English assessor. This Institute of the assessor is mentioned in the English Arbitration Act where it says the tribunal may appoint assessors to assist it on technical matters. When Michael E. Schneider and I tried to find out more about this Institute and how it works in practice, we had also the assistance of Phillip Capper who was nice enough to provide a note but at the end we had to note that there is not much out there so we would be grateful for any input from the floor. So far the only definition that seems to be out there is that he is the one who does not write a report so it would be interesting to see what his precise task is.

Another innovative approach regarding assistance to the tribunal is expert teaming, also referred to as the Sachs Protocol. Expert teaming goes back to a paper presented by Dr Klaus Sachs in 2010. It is a hybrid approach between party-appointed experts and a tribunal-appointed expert. It wants to avoid possible problems also arising from the use of party-appointed experts, namely hugely diverging results in the different reports, and problems arising from using a tribunal-appointed expert, which is the parties feel they cannot control his relation with the tribunal.

The main features of expert teaming are the following. At an early stage of the proceeding the tribunal invites the parties to each provide a short list of candidates from which the tribunal chooses two experts, one from each list, and appoints them as an expert team. Based on the terms of a protocol established with the tribunal and the parties the expert team then prepares its own report.

I spoke to Dr Sachs a few days ago about his personal experience with expert teaming and he said he has used the instrument of expert teaming in five or six cases. Using expert teaming in practice has apparently shown that the team building between the experts works well. In all of the cases the expert team presented a joint opinion. The experts also seem to enjoy the confidence of the party who has nominated them, at least in the beginning of the proceedings, which is an advantage over a tribunal-appointed expert. As a last point, experience shows that expert teaming is particularly suited for very technical issues where there is not much room for interpretation.

Another form of assistance to arbitral tribunals discussed in recent years is that of a special master. The term special master comes from US litigation. Special masters may be appointed by US Federal judges to oversee one or more aspects of the litigation. They have been appointed for accounting or for the calculation of damages. Recently they have been used more often in the administration and distribution of large funds in civil class actions.

Another typical task of a special master is managing document production. Using document production managers in arbitration will be the subject of Hans van Houtte's presentation. At this point I would like to mention only two things: first of all, given the size and complexity of some of today's arbitrations, and class arbitration becoming a reality, it seems worthwhile to examine the institute of the special master more closely to see what it could bring to complex arbitrations.

Secondly, as existing arbitration laws and rules still focus on a more traditional expert role, the task of a special master and how he is requested to proceed should be laid out in sufficient detail in his Terms of Reference after close consultation with the parties.

Coming to our next point, assistance may also come from the permanent staff of an institution. Let me go direct to the less common forms of assistance provided by institutions. An interesting form of assistance is that of the permanent secretariat of the arbitration board for the building industry in The Netherlands. Another less common form of assistance can be found at the United Nations Compensation Committee with its permanent staff of experts. Geoffrey Senogles will tell us more about the UNCC in his presentation.

As for the arbitration board of the building industry, the Raad van Arbitrage voor de Bouw, I chose to include it in this overview because it is an interesting example of the interplay between a tribunal composed of non-lawyers and legally trained staff of the secretariat. I have to say I already got a critical feedback on the workings of the institution so I am looking forward to discussing this afterwards.

I discussed the procedure before the board a few days ago with its director and was told that the board handles more than 1,000 disputes from the building industry every year. The rules provide for first instance and appeal proceedings. A tribunal of first instance, and that is the interesting part, is normally composed of three non-lawyers from the industry unless appointing a lawyer is *"desirable due to the nature of the dispute"*.

Every tribunal is assisted by a legally trained secretary drawn from the institution's permanent staff. The secretary has the task to advise the tribunal in legal matters and to draft the award. After the hearing the secretary sits down with the arbitrators and discusses the claims. The arbitrators tell the secretary how they wish to decide each claim and it is the task of the secretary to make sure that the decision is based on clear and consistent reasoning. If the reasoning is not clear, the secretary will ask questions to establish the arbitrators' motivation, and on that basis he will then draft the award.

We now go back to standard commercial arbitration. Assistance by the institution will usually not go beyond administering the arbitration. Thus, the tribunal may want to seek the help of a secretary, usually a younger associate in the chairman's firm. Emotions run high with this topic and some practitioners seem to deeply distrust this form of assistance. I leave you to Zachary Douglas and our later discussion to tackle the reasons for this distrust and how to deal with it.

In this first round I would like to focus on the potential tasks of the secretary. Before that, however, let me briefly address the appointment of the secretary.

If arbitration rules are silent on the appointment of secretaries it is best practice that tribunals will ask the parties whether they agree with the appointment. This practice is also reflected in the new ICC notes on administrative secretaries.

It is also generally accepted that the secretary must satisfy the same independence and impartiality requirements as arbitrators do. This strict requirement seems to recognise that the secretary's role is not limited to sorting the files; clearly there is more to it.

Moving on to the tasks of the secretary, there is wide consensus that they include administrative tasks. Such tasks typically are organisation of the file of hearings and meetings and taking notes and minutes. However, not much has been said about whether the use of a legally trained secretary for administrative matters is in all cases efficient. I would like to submit for discussion whether at least some of the organisational tasks such as the booking of conference rooms, court reporters, catering and so on would not be in better hands with the chairman's administrative staff or that of parties' counsel.

If we now look at non-administrative tasks, a useful tool for an arbitrator may be chronologies of facts and abstracts, summarising the parties' positions and the evidence offered so allowing the arbitrator to navigate through the file more quickly. However, this is also an area of concern. You must be clear that any work product prepared by the secretary does not release the arbitrator from her duty to personally review the file. Summaries provided by the secretary may be incomplete or contain mistakes. The arbitrator must be able to detect such flaws based on her own detailed knowledge of the file.

Another area in which a secretary's assistance is useful is legal research and this is now recognised by the ICC. The secretary will often prepare memoranda outlining the status of the discussion in case law and legal literature preferably together with copies of the discussed law materials. Since the secretary is not supposed to assume any decision-making functions I expect the memoranda do be limited to an abstract legal discussion leaving it to the arbitrator to apply the law to the facts.

As for the role of the secretary in the drafting of awards, there seems to be growing support that the secretary may draft certain or formal uncontroversial sections of the award but for anything beyond that, opinions are greatly divided. Some say a secretary may very well draft an award if he does it upon detailed instructions of the tribunal; others find this notion shocking because they feel that writing is part of the thinking process.

One approach I have seen in practice which works well in my view is the arbitrator setting out in writing the structure of the award and the line of argumentation including the reference to the relevant evidence. The secretary would then fill in the gaps, which means complete the citations, adding the exact references and so on but not adding any points of substance.

As to procedural orders I think one should take into account that they are often much less complex than awards which raise, at least for some procedural orders, the issue whether the role of the secretary can go further here than it goes with awards.

I hope this overview has served the purpose to prepare to ground for the next presentation and our discussion on the many interesting questions related to this topic. Thank you for your attention.

MICHAEL E.SCHNEIDER:

We will now hear Hans van Houtte whom you all know. Amongst his many functions I mention the one he is occupying now, that is the chair of the Iran-US Claims Tribunal, another institution where there is an important contribution of the Secretariat to the finding of the decisions. What he is talking to us about is not the Iran-US Claims Tribunal but one of his inventions, the document production master and the experts' facilitator.

Document Production Master and Experts' Facilitator

Hans van Houtte

HANS VAN HOUTTE:

Ladies and gentlemen, dear organisers, thank you for inviting me to take the floor. I could have said a lot about dissenting opinions because the Iran-US Clams Tribunal is the champion of dissenting opinions but that is not my topic. I will briefly discuss two types of persons, who can assist the arbitrators in the arbitration process, and who I described in more detail in a paper.[1]

The first person is the "document production master." Document production has become a substantial element in arbitration. Even in arbitration between exclusively continental European parties with continental European arbitrators, document production has become quite important. However, document production sometimes substantially complicates the arbitration process. The IBA Rules on evidence allude to the problems which may arise. Of course, there is the danger of fishing expeditions, which can easily be blocked by the arbitrators. More delicate is the question whether documents are relevant or whether the production of documents constitutes an unreasonable burden, when the arbitrators are not familiar with the documents. And what to do with confidential or privileged documents: should they be excluded from production or edited and sanitised?

Arbitrators can cope with those issues but it will take them some time and require thorough investigation, while very often decisions on document production need to be reached within a short time frame and arbitrators may not be available on short notice to meticulously examine the production request. A specific hearing to discuss document production may be difficult to arrange and entails substantial travel, time and expenses. The biggest problem, however, is the knowledge the arbitrators will keep of documents which they did not admit because of privilege or confidentiality. Human beings are no computers where text disappears from memory by simply using the delete key.

---

[1] Hans van Houtte, The Document Production Master and the Experts' Facilitator, Liber Amicorum Bernardo Cremades, 2010, pp. 1147-1159.

That is where the "document production master" enters the scene. (The WIPO arbitration rules (Art. 52, d) refer to him as the "confidentiality adviser" and the IBA Rules on the Taking of Evidence Art. 38, allow for the appointment of a "production expert").

Some time ago, an Arbitral Tribunal of the Permanent Court of Arbitration had to decide the boundary dispute between British Guyana and Suriname. The Tribunal asked me to go through the confidential archives of the Ministry of Foreign Affairs of the Netherlands (the former colonial ruler of Suriname) to select and sanitize the relevant document (the dispute concerned only the land border and not the sea border — which also was in dispute but not yet subject of arbitral settlement). With the approval of the Tribunal, I decided that also the documents related to the border between Suriname and its neighbour to the East, French Guyana, would be relevant as — in my view — there had to be some consistency between the principles the Dutch colonial power applied to the neighbour of the West and to the neighbour to the East. The modalities of this exercise as "document production master" can be found in the Award.[2]

The second figure I would like to discuss is the "expert co-ordinator." Party-appointed experts are generally preferred above tribunal experts for different reasons. First of all, the selection of a tribunal expert is very delicate. The selection of a court expert largely affects the outcome of his expertise as most experts have a predetermined pattern of thinking. Moreover, it is more difficult for the tribunal to dissociate itself from the findings of an expert it has appointed than from the findings of party-appointed experts.

However, party-appointed experts may become "two ships passing in the night" when their reports do not relate to each other. Sometimes their reports, moreover, are not flexible enough so that if one of their assumed parameters (e.g. the interest rate) changes, their extensive findings and calculations become useless.

That is where the "expert co-ordinator" enters the scene. Some time ago, I was chairing a tribunal with seat in Oman, where the arbitration statute obliged arbitrators to render a decision within six months, with the possibility of one six months extension. The dispute concerned the construction of a road. In order to issue the award within one year, the Tribunal did not take any risk with the experts: on the day of the hearing the experts had to be ready with useful reports and relevant conclusions. To avoid the "ships passing in the night", the Tribunal therefore appointed an "expert co-ordinator" "with the task to constantly monitor the respective experts and make sure that they

---

[2] Award Guyana v. Suriname, September 17, 2007, Cases Nos. 47-102, www.pca.cpa.org.

were doing their job, keeping their deadlines and answering each other's arguments without overlaps or gaps. The "expert coordinator" had to bring them to a joint report (with "hot-tubbing") so that at the day of the hearing, the Tribunal had the maximum benefit from their findings.

The "expert co-ordinator" should operate independently from the tribunal. He is more like a school teacher who has to make sure that the pupils do their homework in a convenient way and, prepare them for the exam.

The "document production-master" and the "expert coordinator" can be of great help for arbitrators to make the proceedings more efficient and thus save expenses.

MICHAEL E. SCHNEIDER:

We will now turn to Zachary Douglas. Zachary has many different hats. He is a professor now for International Law at the Graduate Institute in Geneva. He is also a barrister and an arbitrator. He will look into the subject we are all familiar with, the secretary to the tribunal, and speak to some of the experiences he had with this peculiar institution.

The Secretary to the Arbitral Tribunal

Zachary Douglas

ZACHARY DOUGLAS:

The odds are stacked up against us a little bit today. We are running late; this is one of the final sessions; the winter light outside is fading; red wine was served at lunchtime; all sorts of things. As a professor I have a lot of experience of sending an audience to sleep. What you did not see at the back of the room is that there are two rows of my students in the room nodding as I'm saying this so my attempt at irony has fallen flat on its face!

I am going to try to enlighten you on a single question: is it legitimate for a secretary or assistant to the tribunal to draft the tribunal's award in whole or in part. I want to introduce this topic with a story, which is partly fact, partly fiction.

Here comes the true part of the story: Just over a year ago after I moved to Geneva I received a CV applying for the job of assistant to me. I always think when I get these CVs that times must be tough because I have never advertised for such a position nor have I ever hired an assistant. Nonetheless, I opened the attachment out of curiosity and one thing caught my eye immediately. There was a heading with the formulation "Awards that I have drafted". I had never heard of this person before but I looked down the list of awards that he had drafted and, surprise surprise, one of the awards was in a case in which I appeared as counsel. Immediately one thinks about an obligation to pass on this information to the former client and so on but I will leave that to one side.

I suspect many of us have received CVs like that. There is a human nature element you can understand. That candidate went too far in selling his profile but you can understand the dilemma. You have spent three or four years acting in that capacity for someone very senior and you are trying to get another job. Unless you can convey the full extent of your experience then you will be prejudiced in a very competitive market for associate positions at law firms and so on.

Here is where my story moves from fact to fiction. Suppose the CV is forwarded to the party who lost. It is a major case where hundreds of millions were paid out in satisfaction of the award. The seat of the arbitration is New York and a challenge proceeding is launched there. The person who drafted the award is now doing an LLM at NYU and he is subpoenaed and has to give evidence. The party resisting the challenge may well think it is a good idea to line up a string of experts to attest to the fact that this practice is so widespread it cannot be criticised. The party making the challenge may counter by introducing expert evidence on, say, the ICC note on administrative secretaries. That note envisages that a secretary to a tribunal performs a purely administrative role.

Such a challenge would be very damaging—and I am talking of the perfect storm—to the reputation of international arbitration. We have had challenges on this basis in the past. There have been cases before the French and German courts. There was a famous case in the Iran-US Claims Tribunal where there was an internal challenge relating to the role of a secretary but we have not had this perfect storm.

The best argument for challenging this award—and it comes back to the true part of the story—is that the role of the secretary was not disclosed to the parties. The best basis for this challenge would be that if this practice of allowing secretaries to draft awards is legitimate then why was it done in secret? Why did the parties not know about it? Why was this not reflected in the award?

This is the crux of the point I want to make. Whether or not this practice of obtaining assistance to write awards should be condemned or encouraged—I think it is quite a complex issue and I will come on to pros and cons in a minute—there are real dangers posed by the lack of transparency. The bottom line is that parties need information about how a tribunal proposes to produce its award in order to make an informed choice at the outset of the proceedings.

Before I talk about the pros and cons, why has this become an acute problem? It has been mentioned throughout the day and it is to do with the professionalisation of arbitration and the effect on the arbitrator's role. Parties are deploying massive resources in fighting their corner in international arbitrations with the result that the quantity of the evidential materials and the length of the written pleadings are overwhelming tribunals comprising of one or three human beings with less than twenty-four hours in a day to devote to a particular case. In one case I am involved in, thankfully as counsel, it would take an arbitrator 292 days (assuming a 12-hour working day and 3 minutes to read a page) to review the exhibits filed by one of the parties in one of the rounds of written submissions… Arbitrating, in turn, has become more specialised and increasingly many people do make a living out of being a full-time arbitrator—which was not the case twenty years ago. Unlike a national court judge, an arbitrator needs a critical mass of cases before abandoning other parts of his or her legal practice but once that critical mass is attained it is exceedingly difficult for an individual to manage that caseload. There is a lot said about arbitrators having a no basis for complaint because they have complete discretion whether or not to take on cases. In reality, however, if you have the critical mass of cases needed to be taken seriously as a professional arbitrator, a great deal of things are beyond your control. Cases settle, filings get postponed, extensions are granted and hearings get pushed back. For instance, the amount of time that an arbitrator originally reserved to digest pleadings running into hundreds of pages before a hearing may suddenly evaporate because the parties in another case have agreed to alter their schedule.

In light of this professionalization of arbitration, it is perhaps surprising that we are still wedded to the idea of the lone arbitrator sitting among a mass of files and papers in a stuffy office somewhere churning out flawless legal prose with a fountain pen.

It is interesting that some of the very senior arbitrators, who we know rely upon junior assistants quite substantially to draft their awards, are still appointed time and time again. This is happening because the senior arbitrators I have in mind are being transparent about it and some users of arbitration are prepared to accept that they will not have the assurance of the chairperson or the co-arbitrators drafting every sentence of the award. They are prepared to accept that because they know it will lead to a faster resolution of their dispute. How many times have you heard a business person say: "we do not care what the decision is, we just need a decision". I suspect that there are limits to that rhetoric but the point is that justice delayed can be justice denied. It is also curious that sophisticated parties are prepared to fund the presentation of a written record that is so voluminous that only a fraction of it will actually be read by the arbitrators. Are they counting on assistants to the tribunal doing some of the heavy lifting behind the scenes? Or are they counting on the members of the tribunal clearing the 292 days necessary in their diary to review the exhibits attached to a single pleading?

I say all this despite being a fervent believer that the act of writing is the ultimate safeguard of intellectual control over the decision-making process. I personally resist delegating any writing but I have come to appreciate that this is not the only legitimate way to serve the parties' interests in an arbitration.

As I said before, the bottom line is that the users of arbitration need to know more about how the tribunal proposes to render its award. There needs to be transparency. It is very difficult to see how this is going to be implemented but here is a modest proposal. There are obvious problems with it but what is no longer sustainable is to continue with the mythology about the lone arbitrator who never resorts to any assistance in any circumstances.

This proposal actually comes from my experience in being interviewed as a potential arbitrator in investment treaty cases. It seems like "beauty parades" are increasingly the norm for these appointments and I have been subjected to this on several occasions. One question that is often asked is: what is your position on assistance to the tribunal? On the basis of the candidate's response, the party can make an informed decision about whether to nominate that co-arbitrator.

The critical person in this equation is the chair. How do you instil this transparency in relation to the appointment of the chair? We all understand that if you are going to give the parties a choice it cannot be after the tribunal is appointed for very obvious reasons; obvious at least to this audience.

How do you go about ensuring this happens? When the candidate is put forward and that person is making the usual disclosures relating to conflicts of interest and so on, one could conceive of a system whereby that chairperson, perhaps in consultation with the co-arbitrators but before he or she is appointed, comes up with a proposal as to what assistance is going to be used and also comes up with a fee structure for that assistance. That disclosure or that proposal goes to the parties, they have an opportunity to consider it, and then they make representations as to whether or not they find it acceptable to the institution. I am assuming there is an institution managing the arbitration. Then it would probably be up to the institution to decide whether or not to go forward with the particular candidate in light of those representations from the parties.

We probably need to have a change of the common arbitration rules. I think the real danger now is that there is such a gulf between the official position on display in the ICC note and in the ubiquitous reference to the secretary's role as being purely administrative in the common arbitration rules, on the one hand, and what is actually happening in practice, on the other.

There are several other issues which also need to be addressed but time is not on my side today. Costs are a big point. Clearly there must be a distinction between arbitrations where the costs are assessed on an *ad valorem* basis and an arbitration where the arbitrators are remunerated on the basis of an hourly rate. The ICC has taken the view that the cost of administrative assistants should not come as an additional cost to the parties. That is a position that is difficult to fault given the way that costs are assessed in ICC arbitrations but it may be different where arbitrators are remunerated on the basis of an hourly rate.

To conclude, I expect people will have strong views on this issue and I look forward to an interesting discussion. Having now had the privilege of sitting with many of the senior arbitrators I have come to understand that one's views depend to a large extent on one's culture of legal practice. I am a barrister. I have spent most of my career being instructed in my individual capacity. If writing is to be delegated by a barrister then the person in question must generally come onto the record of the case and his or her name must appear on the pleadings and will be noted in the judgment. People with a different culture of legal practice may be more or less inclined to delegate and also be more or less adept at delegating. Delegation is both an art and a science and barristers are notoriously bad at it. It is a cultural thing.

Thank you very much for the invitation. This is my first ASA conference and I have thoroughly enjoyed it. Thank you for your attention.

MICHAEL E. SCHNEIDER:

Thank you very much both for your presentation and for your proposal. You have seen me talking for a moment to Hans because I had a sudden idea whether I wanted Hans to give us an input on the institution which is probably the one, at least from the outside, where secretaries have the biggest role in drafting. He said he did not want to talk about this but I see Douglas Reichert in the room who was at the Secretariat of the Iran-US Claims Tribunal so I will call on him in a moment. I warn him in advance.

In the meantime Geoff is a non-lawyer but has been very much involved with our legal work, in particular in the United Nations Compensation Commission. We thought it would be useful to have his experience because it is about the opposite of the paradigm we know. It is perhaps the institution that went furthest in giving assistance and outside input into what, in that institution was the panel, into the panel decision.

The United Nations Compensation Commission's Utilisation of Experts

Geoffrey Senogles

GEOFFREY SENOGLES:

It is a privilege to be here particularly as the only non-lawyer who has spoken today. I am an accountant, I apologise! My core practice is international arbitration as an expert witness. I have been asked to speak today thinking back ten years to my time in the United Nations Compensation Commission in Geneva, so this is all old news.

For those who do not know much about the UNCC, please bear with me. I am going to spend a few minutes giving you some context of what we were doing and why. Shown on the screen are the dates of the invasion and occupation, a period of seven months almost 22 years ago. Where was each of us on 2 August 1990?

At a glance; the United States Compensation Commission was established by the Security Council as a part of the Security Council. Some of the biggest numbers that I think need to be kept in mind and, as we have discussed as a panel, we are not saying the UNCC is like an ICC or ICSID tribunal, clearly it is not. There is a very clear distinction.

There were over 2.5 million claims filed in all, with a total asserted value of just over US$350 billion. The bulk of the claims were at the personal level: death, injury and damage to property. The larger claims are shown on the bottom line of the slide on the screen: commercial, governmental and environmental.

Do not worry, I know what it is like presenting to tribunals; nobody likes a page full of numbers. All this information is available on the UNCC website; it is fully transparent and sets out the 13 categories of claims. To save your eyesight these are some of the key elements: 2.7 million claims, of those claims 1.5 million were deemed successful, therefore were proved to the satisfaction of the panels of commissioners. The compensation sought, as I mentioned, was over US$350 billion and of that, US$52 billion was awarded. There are some pretty significant figures here. The average award is just less than 15%. If you take out the single largest award, that percentage comes down to roughly 10%. There was one exceptionally large award of US$17 billion awarded to Kuwait Petroleum Corporation.

Of the amount awarded almost US$39 billion has been paid to date. This is a UN agency that has really delivered some tangible impact. In fact, these figures are probably slightly out of date because payments are made on a quarterly basis and these are taken from the website as at 25 October 2012 so there should have been a payment made in the past few days; roughly US$1 billion is paid per quarter. You can see as at the figures available US$13 billion is still payable.

I am going to skate through these because this is not the point of the panel but I want to give you some context. Some people here know a lot about it, for others it will be new. The governing council of the UNCC was the primary body that was a mirror image of the Security Council: 15 members, permanent five and then ten member countries on a rotation. 19 separate panels of commissioners. For the sharp-eyed people in the room you will remember there were 13 categories of claim and 19 panels. Each panel had three commissioners.

The Secretariat when I was there, at the peak, was 250 people (about the same number as the people who started here this morning to give you an idea of the scale of the operation), and it was based in the Palais des Nations, Geneva.

Panels of commissioners; there were 19 separate panels, three on each. We would regard them now as a tribunal but we never used that term in the Secretariat. We never used the term tribunal; it was the panel.

I am playing to my audience here but the overwhelming majority of commissioners were lawyers, typically very experienced arbitrators. There were also non-lawyers, the brave people like me here today, accountants, loss adjusters and an insurer.

Support to each panel of commissioners was split into two: staff members and external consultants. Just to prove my *bona fides*, I have kept my old UN passport [shown]. The staff for each panel was divided between essentially lawyers and a valuation person. The team leader was always a lawyer. Each claim was assigned to a senior lawyer and sometimes on the particularly large claims there would be more than one lawyer responsible. A valuation person like myself would be assigned to the team. I was assigned to several teams because I was the only forensic accountant on the valuation staff.

The external consultants always included forensic accountants. Also to the extent necessary there were property, asset and valuation experts. We had loss adjustors. There were many different gas and petroleum experts, petroleum engineers, gas pricing, oil pricing, the refinery engineers and economists..

We have heard today about the black box. I am going to be different. The UN we all know uses the colour blue so I am going to call it the blue box. Each panel typically met each month in the Palais des Nations over two or three days. The claims were presented inside the blue box. They were presented by the lawyer and the valuation person would assist.

Certain claims were designated large and complex and that is when the mass processing machine, if you like, was substituted for a more line by line assessment by the panels and the support team advisers (both internal and external).

The external consultants were contracted by instalments so a group of similar claims using the typical UN process, always a forensic accounting firm and the other experts were brought in as and when needed.

Again, we are inside the box. The point of today is really to explore how did the panel of Commissioners receive information, receive advice, on which to base their decisions? The external experts or external consultants would work very closely with the Secretariat team (legal and valuation) who would make sure that the expert consultants knew the methodologies and any particular issues

The Secretariat team and the external consultants would review the claim documents submitted. As in almost every case clarification questions were drafted both by the Secretariat and external consultants and were sent to the claimants. The claim file was sent to Iraq for comments. Do not forget Iraq was not specifically represented but they were able to provide comments; and they were very good, very useful comments.

In particular instances, particularly on the large and complex claims, we would go on site visits. We spent a great deal of time in the Persian Gulf and elsewhere inspecting refineries, all kinds of different businesses that were impacted, and government ministries. Again, to summarise the process, the experts went with the Secretariat.

I am trying to give you a flavour of the process. The valuation staff would assist the panel with any particular issues that were relevant to it. The external consultants would present their opinion to the panel typically in a draft report format but also orally in meetings. This was a highly interactive process and would continue over several meetings on large and complex claims.

The panel would ask questions. It was a very open process and the panel would ask questions of the experts. The experts would give their independent opinion to the panel in writing and, as I say, this process would go on over several months, several meetings, until the panel were satisfied with the report that was drafted.

For certain claims, typically those over US$1 billion in value, all hearings were convened at the Palais des Nations. There are some claimant names shown on the slide on the screen – I was involved in all of those listed. The claimant was represented by counsel and by technical experts and Iraq was represented in the same way.

Again, these are truncated hearings. These are not a week's hearing for one claim. They could be half a day or a day. The largest value claim in the UNCC was submitted by the sovereign wealth fund of Kuwait, asserted at approximately US$85 billion. The hearing on that claim took place on 12 September 2001; a one-day hearing. The day before that, September 11, I was involved in other hearings on two oil sector claims. I am trying to illustrate that the UNCC process was not the same as a commercial or investment treaty arbitration.

Each panel report was drafted by the legal team but it was, in my experience, edited word by word and line by line, by the panel members. It took time but once again, the key point I am making is that the decision making was in the hands of the commissioners. Yes, there was assistance and analysis in support, but the decision was in the hands of the panel.

Once the panel report was signed, it was considered by the Governing Council. If they voted their approval then the Panel's report was published on the UNCC website [www.uncc.ch] and payments would follow.

Very briefly, and finally, for those environmental claims that were awarded compensation, the Governing Council required that a team of independent reviewers be appointed to follow up on the amounts awarded. As it happens, I am one of those independent reviewers. Our team is a multidisciplinary team of a dozen or so international experts on financial, technical and scientific issues and our mandate is to report to the Governing Council. We are contracted by the claimant State to monitor and provide guidance on the implementation of the awards.

That is a very brief overview of the UNCC and I hope it has been of some interest.

MICHAEL E. SCHNEIDER:

Thank you for your insight into a procedure that very few of you will have to encounter in the future as hopefully we will not have this type of war where it was applied.

Two comments: one of the remarkable features was the speed and the number of awards that were made especially in the early stages of the process. The small claims were dealt with up-front. There were one million Egyptian workers in Iraq who were claiming their money which had been blocked; in a very short time the panel made a decision. The type of misgivings we can have about a process like this, if the upside is that these workers got their money in a relatively short period, I think that is something to be considered.

The other point concerns the hearings. We had on some of the environmental claims six governments claiming US$30 billion and we had four hours to argue the case. It is an extremely useful discipline. You have to rehearse that several times but what you learn about concentration of your case I think is an experience which every practising lawyer, and all those lawyers who appear before us with long speeches, should go through. I think it is a very useful discipline.

The first thing I would like to ask Hans as one of the Commissioners is to tell us about this interaction. How does a panellist keep his independence of judgment, the sovereignty of his judgment, if you have such a degree of input of people who are not part of the panel, who are the Secretariat and the outside experts?

HANS VAN HOUTTE:

I fully agree with Geoff. The UNCC heavily relied on experts but that may be explained by the specific character of the whole UNCC system. For instance, when a set of claims was submitted to a Panel, it needed to render its decision within exactly 12 months. That practically excluded the Panel investigating the facts in detail. It had to rely substantially on experts.

Moreover, experts were useful to check the facts and numbers, alleged by Claimant, because the Respondent, Iraq, initially did not make adequate use of the possibility to address the claims, but limited itself to general political objections. The Panels furthermore were not allowed to investigate on site the local reality but were obliged to rely on the second-hand information from staff members. In spite of all these constraints the Commissioners, experts and staff members did a fair and honest job in thoroughly examining the claims. For instance, the F2 Panel, of which I was a member, granted only 72 million USD of the 8 billion USD Jordan had claimed (*i.e.* only 0,8%).

It has to be admitted: the UNCC Panels were not truly independent arbitral tribunals. UNCC team leaders attended the deliberations and, if ever a Panel went in a direction not taken by other Panels, it was politely reminded that it decided differently from what other Panels had done. Moreover, Panel decisions were only "recommendations" and had to be submitted to the Governing Council, which had the last word. Nevertheless, within the political and diplomatic context of the UNCC, the Panels performed fairly and meticulously.

MICHAEL E. SCHNEIDER:

The critical point was how does one stay independent? Is it your decision or is it something of a big institution where you are one making a contribution together with the others?

HANS VAN HOUTTE:

It is rather the second proposition. However, within the UNCC on our level, we decided independently.

MICHAEL E. SCHNEIDER:

I had announced to Douglas that, since Hans does not want to talk about this, can you give us a short explanation about the role of the secretary in the Iran-US Claims Tribunal in the earlier days where I think they played a particularly important role?

DOUGLAS REICHERT:

I am not the only person in the room today who has lived in The Hague and worked in the Iran-US Claims Tribunal so others could also speak. I have been living throughout my legal career inside the black box, which I just realised a moment ago, because, coming out of law school, I joined the staff of the Iran-US Claims Tribunal, where of course it was not completely transparent. Each member of the tribunal had a legal assistant and I was hired as a legal assistant, which is something quite different from a secretary of a commercial arbitration tribunal. There were Chamber Clerks also in the Secretariat of this institution, who performed the administrative role equivalent to a secretary of a commercial arbitration.

As Hans van Houtte emphasised, it was a different tribunal in those days. I could also add that I think it was nearly thirty years ago when I, still as a law student, was able to attend one of the hearing sessions of this tribunal, basically based on the provision that we saw this morning on one of the slides about ICSID rules requiring that no-one outside the proceedings could participate in a hearing unless the tribunal would decide otherwise. I happened to be passing through The Hague at that time and the tribunal was asked if they would tolerate having an outsider present in the hearing session and they very kindly allowed me to get a first glimpse at that time.

I can add that I stayed inside the black box because after The Hague Tribunal I was the Registrar of the Egypt-Israel Arbitration Tribunal. There as the Registrar I had a function modelled upon that of the International Court of Justice, where the Registrar of the International Court of Justice is a part of the process inside the black box.

I must say when you are inside the black box, and I am sure many of you have this experience, the world looks perfectly normal; it is when you are outside the box that it is quite different. It is only recently in my practice that I have been outside the box looking in, wondering what they are doing and are they doing it the way I think they might be doing it but I certainly cannot be sure about that. I was not expecting to learn today from Hans van Houtte that inside the black box there can be another black box, and that is the document production master who you might give the process to, so that you do not have to see the documents.

The role of the legal assistants in the Iran-US Claims Tribunal at that time was like a fly on the wall. I had the privilege of seeing how it happened, but in the particular chamber in which I worked it was a language issue. This is a bilingual tribunal, the Farsi language and the English language, and not all of the members were at that time in that particular experience fully fluent in both languages, and so for the deliberative process they would be relying on their legal assistants to express their point of view in the deliberation so that the other members of the panel could understand what their contribution was. There were a variety of roles that the assistant to each member had at the Iran-US Claims Tribunal.

We were just reminded today it is still functioning, but with an inter-State process only, and for the benefit of that process the black box is necessary and useful.

MICHAEL E. SCHNEIDER:

What was the role of the assistant to the chairman in the drafting of the decisions?

DOUGLAS REICHERT:

Since I was not an assistant to the chairman I cannot say.

MICHAEL E. SCHNEIDER:

Before we speak about problems and particular aspects, is there in the room anybody who has had similar experiences other than the ones we spoke about where the assistant to the tribunal made major contributions. Can you tell us about the way how they handled the case and in the way how the tribunal reached its decision?

JACOMIJN VAN HAERSOLTE-VAN HOF:

I had one experience that I thought of when Andrea was describing the assessor and I think that may have been the basis for the experience. I was appointed assistant, adviser, expert to an expert. It was an expert determination situation where there was a terrified accountant who had been appointed as expert in a determination under English law he thought but it was under Dutch law.

He discovered that the rules under Dutch law are quite different. For instance, he would have to give reasons which he was not used to. What the parties, in their wisdom, decided was to provide the man with an adviser, or a baby sitter I should say. I sat through this entire procedure holding his hand and saying "This is relevant. There is an issue of Dutch law that you should be aware of. You should apply due process." It was complicated by the fact that it was an expert determination which does not have quite the legal status of arbitration. It worked well but unfortunately he died before he could give his decision but the process was quite successful!

PATRICK HEHENBERGER:

As I look around I am probably one of the very few experts in this room. As you talk about baby sitters, I certainly do not need any babysitting when I do my contributions in arbitral proceedings as an expert either appointed by the parties or by the tribunal.

My first observation goes to the important point of getting the interface right between the technical engineer and the arbitral tribunal in such a way that there is no overlap and no gap left between one and the other. This is in the sense of avoiding any loss of time and energy and therefore costs to both parties.

I think it is of great value to choose an expert who has the technical background in technical matters to establish the facts and to analyse and to explain these facts and who, at the same time, understands the legal background and the legal issues at stake. Then he can ensure that he goes right to that interface between the expert and the arbitral tribunal.

My second remark, which is related to this, goes to the writing of the expert report, and the communication between the expert and the tribunal. It is of great help to know what degree of technical knowledge is available in the arbitral tribunal. If you do not know what they know, you may spend a lot of time telling them things pointlessly or you may just not keep in touch with them appropriately. I think it is important to enable a distinguished communication between the expert and the arbitral tribunal and it is for the expert to ensure that he, again, gets to that point where he is most efficient in the process and that you do not need secondary counter-expertise and no further rounds for more questions and delays in the arbitral process.

MICHAEL E. SCHNEIDER:

Any other experiences of such outside support?

CRENGUTA LEAUA:

I was thinking maybe you had such an experience, but in a very different role than the ones mentioned here. I am thinking now about the scrutiny role the ICC Court is performing as far as the drafting of the arbitral awards is concerned. That is an interesting role that might be outside the scope of the subject of this conference but maybe not as outside as it may look like, at least in the process of drafting the award.

MICHAEL E. SCHNEIDER:

That is a very interesting question to which I cannot respond because I never sat on the Court but I know in the room there are quite a number of people who have sat on the Court. I can see as an arbitrator the type of things that come back and the type of changes that are made to the award or can be made further to the intervention of the Court and this is totally black box. I know that the parties are not informed about the types of observations that are made by the Court and the type of changes that are made to awards. Is there somebody who sat on the Court who will help us understand this process?

MARKUS WIRTH:

As far as the scrutiny of awards by the ICC is concerned, there is also some sort of a black box for the members of the Court sitting either on a committee or in the plenary session as one gets the comments of the Secretariat on the awards before they are discussed. How the Secretariat gets to its comments, and who is involved in that process is sometimes not very clear.

MICHAEL E. SCHNEIDER:

The experience I have, and what I hear from others, is that the observations are not just commas and spelling. The observations, even though the rules say recommendations as to form, the substance of the comments can be quite far reaching. I hear some of the justifications for the role of the Court that some of the awards that get to the Court are abominable and require substantial improvement but that means there is a large input into the award from the Court.

MARKUS WIRTH:

I can confirm that. However, you do not have that much time as a Court member or a member of a committee to go through each and every draft award that is presented. Sometimes you get two binders of decisions and draft awards just four or five working days before the session.

I think what most of the Court members do is they look for black holes in the awards. Are there relevant points missing in terms of either the factual presentation or the application of the law? The second thing you are looking for is contradictions within the awards. And the third one is the quantum and the correctness of the calculations. These are not formal things. These are matters of substance. The usual practice is that where one discovers obvious contradictions, wrong calculations, or black holes, the award is sent back to the arbitrators – but you can do that only so often. If the arbitrators after the third time the draft award has been sent back say "We insist on it" that's it and the award goes out.

MICHAEL E. SCHNEIDER:

My question in return is: is that any different for me as an arbitrator or chairman of the tribunal with the complicated summary in a cable dispute and I call an expert in and tell him "Can you please check my award? Did I get this right or can you help me" or I tell Geoff "I have here a damage calculation. I have heard the experts and made this decision. Can you have a look at it and tell me whether I have something wrong?" He tells me then yes or no but I get it back and the parties do not know about it. Is that any different? That was a rhetorical question.

ERIK SCHÄFER:

I am very confused. Why am I confused? Arbitration is a flexible system. When we talk about what is good practice and bad practice we need to define a standard against which we measure what is good and bad. I propose that we say practice is good if the quality of the work-product has been increased. We should not state that something is good or bad because we do or do not see it in civil procedure which we know from State courts. I really think about increasing the quality of the result that we produce, i.e., the arbitral award. If I have an arbitrator who has many cases on-going, the quality might be increased by somebody who works for the arbitral tribunal in the background and spends days and nights dealing with the case. This somebody usually is a junior lawyer. Thus, I wonder how we can decide whether all these practices we have seen are good or bad? We need to define the standards first before we look into these practices to see whether we want them or not.

MICHAEL E. SCHNEIDER:

That is why we are trying to give you the wide range. Some of the improvement is that you as an arbitrator do not take the technical information, for instance by saying this expert is credible and this one is not, but by trying to understand and have help in the understanding and thereby improve the award in the technical quality. You have secretaries who draft the award because the arbitrators or the chairman speaks offshore English and that is one of the important contributions, the drafting in the sense, but there goes more into it. That may be a quality element but then the problem is it is happening unknown to the parties and that was the point of Zachary saying you have to have transparency.

REINMAR WOLFF:

Directly jumping into that question of quality, that is certainly an important factor but it is difficult for me to believe that it is the only factor given that we have discussed an entire day today about the efforts that legitimately are spent on appointment procedures, selection of arbitrators, on the balance of powers within tribunals, et cetera, et cetera. It is not only about a good—whatever good means—outcome but rather about a proper procedure to reach whatever outcome.

Zachary has suggested transparency as a measure to do away with the dishonesty problem. That is certainly to be appreciated but is there not the remaining question as to which tasks cannot be delegated? Why do we make such a big effort in selecting arbitrators? Why do we think and discuss so much about how to balance powers within the tribunal when there are third parties appointed in a less legitimate procedure who may have considerable influence on the outcome of the case?

JACOMIJN VAN HAERSOLTE-VAN HOF:

Andrea announced a critical comment. I am not sure if I would like to make a critical comment but I would like to make a comment on your presentation. First of all, I congratulate you on the research having dug up this information on a not obscure but a very specific Dutch institution. I would like to make a few comments on that.

What is interesting about this institution that you described is it is a domestic institution primarily, not exclusively. It has a large number of cases most of which are quite typical and it deals with a particular kind of dispute for which the system that they deploy is quite effective but I would be reluctant to advocate this as an example more broadly.

At the same time, I think it is interesting to review this experience because it comes out of a strong tradition that we have in The Netherlands where secretaries are used. I think in this case, in this particular institution, the secretary is a black box in itself. You do not know who you are getting when you get their legal secretary. You know there will be somebody but you do not know who and that is not something that I would advocate.

Most institutions in The Netherlands, including the Netherlands Arbitration Institute, are entirely transparent about the use of legal secretaries or whatever you call them. They are put to the same standards when it comes to disclosure and potential challenges that are provided in the rules and in the Arbitration Act. The fees are completely transparent. Their fees are ultimately listed as disbursements in the award so you know how many hours are spent. Of course that is after the fact but it will give you some indication of the role of somebody.

The Netherlands Arbitration Institution discusses with the arbitrators and the parties on a case-by-case basis what the needs are. Is it the need for a lawyer if, for instance, the arbitrator is an accountant or an engineer, or is it somebody who will have to do logistical issues because of voluminous document production requests or something. It can be a tailor-made solution.

I was very much intrigued by something Zachary said which is true and not covered under the Dutch system. Typically we appoint somebody after the tribunal is appointed and I do see that it can be a bit difficult to say we refuse to have somebody. I find that because if that discussion is held in the open you can have a fairly honest discussion at least of the profile but also about the need to have a tribunal-appointed secretary or not.

As an NIA arbitrator I work with and without them and it depends on the case. It is very difficult to give you a clear template of the cases that do or do not require a secretary but I am all in favour of transparency and discussing what we want from these people. You do not want to have a decision, like you have in this construction institute, where there is a black box and suddenly somebody has apparently drafted an award that you thought somebody else was going to make.

ANDREA MEIER:

I wanted to shortly say thank you a lot for this practical input and experience about the working of the institution. It seems to me it is very successful and that gives us something to think about that maybe sometimes people estimate when it is an efficient proceeding and they take into account some downsides to the process.

WILLIAM BASSLER:

I want to take this moment to thank you and the Association for allowing me to be a member of this organisation and participate. It has been very enlightening for me.

I think the transparency thing is very important. In the area where I do a lot of my work, which is the American Arbitration Association and its international wing ICDR, the AAA Canon of Ethics permit the use of a legal assistant but it has to be with the approval of counsel. In my experience it is done up-front. There is a résumé of the legal assistant, usually it is a woman at home with children who is a graduate of law school employed by a judge, tremendous experience, and the fees are much less than what the arbitrator would be charging. It has worked very well.

I had two personal experiences with the use of a legal assistant. The first is a very large arbitration in which the parties' counsel themselves offered to each of the three arbitrators a legal assistant. We thought that was an overkill but what we did do was in effect what has been talked about, we had one of the women act for the panel and then we would delegate research projects. Note that I said we delegated research, not the responsibility for making the decision. As a result we got I think a very good product from the panel that we might not otherwise have done if we had tried to do everything ourselves.

The second experience is not so good. I was inexperienced. I was not the chair. We had another arbitrator who thought he was the chair and the parties again offered to have what you call a secretary but basically a legal assistant to help us. I hate to use the word in this group but being an American arbitration we had tons of discovery before we got even into the picture, plus transcripts of trials that counsel wanted us to read. We did not take up the offer; I was outvoted. It was a terrible mistake because we ended up having to read tons of documents in which maybe one or two sentences were of any value to us. Had we had a legal assistant it would have been less expensive and certainly more efficient.

It all depends but I think transparency is really important and I think it can actually end up reducing the cost to the parties if it is done with some sense of responsibility.

ZACHARY DOUGLAS:

What do the AAA Rules say about the scope of the role of an assistant?

WILLIAM BASSLER:

It is not in the rules; it does not say anything. I try to make a practice - I probably do not do it religiously — once a year I try to read the Canon of Ethics of the AAA and it is in the Canon of Ethics which says you may use a legal assistant providing it is done with the consent of counsel and that is all it says. I had been with JAMS and, as I recall, there is nothing in the JAMS rules but I do know that very busy JAMS arbitrators are doing it with the consent of the counsel up-front. The résumé is circulated, they know who the legal assistant is, a conflicts search is done and in my case the assistant signs confidentiality agreements so it can be done.

DAVID HACKING:

In this excellent conference I have one disappointment, and that is nobody has mentioned again the English proverb: "Beware of the demons in the black box". I am going to identify one demon in the black box which is delay: delay by the arbitral tribunal, fixing of the hearings and so forth, and the delay by the parties or their counsel. It is here that I have to draw issue with Zachary Douglas. He was far too kind to the busy arbitrator. He said he knows it is very difficult to run the schedules, that cases settle, that some cases run on too long, but let us look at the facts.

One part of the delay is the delay between the end of the arbitration proceedings and the issue of the award. Again look at the facts which are contained in a survey carried out a few years ago by Allen & Overy in London concerning ICSID arbitrations. What did they find? They found that the average period between the end of the arbitration and the issue of the award was 15 months. More recently Berwin Leighton Paisner has carried out a survey on commercial arbitrations and what did they find? They found that in over 50% of commercial cases that were reported to them as part of the survey the arbitral award was issued over a year from the end of the arbitration proceedings.

Then we turn to what the parties want. We turn to another survey conducted by Phillip Capper's firm and that survey was looking at what did the parties expect. What did they come up with? They had an expectation — I cannot remember the percentage — of three months between the end of the arbitration proceedings and the delivery of the award. Incidentally in London in the Commercial Court that is what has to be explained to the Presiding Judge when a judgment is three months overdue.

MICHAEL E. SCHNEIDER:

Do you think there is help that can be provided? That is the subject of our discussion. Is there any help that would change anything?

DAVID HACKING:

Yes, there are steps to be taken but it has to be taken by the institutions and by the individual arbitrators. What I am drawing attention to is what I have to say is now a scandalous problem of delay between the end of the arbitration proceedings and the issue of the award.

Zachary said that what the parties really wanted was a decision to resolve the dispute rather than looking at waiting for an award. It is more important to get the decision. I cannot give you answers but I can give you the problem.

PIERRE TERCIER:

I would like to make two general comments on what we heard. I will make them both as a professor and as an arbitrator. I consider that we should avoid concluding this discussion on a negative note, especially in view of the fact that many young (future) arbitrators are attending this conference.

My first comment on the "black box" of the deliberation: The expression could be misunderstood and give the impression that what occurs during the deliberation process is something mysterious, suspicious. In fact, this is nothing else than the agreed procedure following which three persons chosen by the parties try to take the best decision, based on the parties' submissions. The task is demanding and challenging, and requires independency, rigor and intense work from each member of the panel. One should avoid placing new burdens on the shoulders of the arbitrators, and to the contrary, find ways to ease their task, which becomes always more cumbersome, complex and massive. What is important is the quality of the end product that comes out of the black box: the award. Indeed the award constitutes the best evidence of the seriousness and the quality of the work accomplished by the arbitrators. The case may be that some arbitrators are not serious and do not act as they should, but it would be a shame to give the wrong impression that it is a common behavior.

My second comment relates to the "black box" of the ICC. The interventions of the ICC are often criticized and the ICC has somewhat been criticized again today. The process may not be perfect, lack transparency, and some proposals from the ICC (editorial or related to the merits) may sometimes be inaccurate. However, having had the opportunity to work a lot with the Court, I can confirm that the contribution of the ICC services are tremendous. The scrutinization process is definitely an added value to the quality of the award. It may of course be improved, but should not be questioned in its principle. Here again, I believe that we ought to conclude on a more positive note.

MICHAEL E. SCHNEIDER:

I thank you very much for this closing statement because it is precisely the purpose of the session here: that we look at the different forms of assistance. As a user of ICC I value very highly this input and to have somebody who has not been involved in the process look over it. I got very useful comments on awards that were sent back.

The purpose of my intervention was not to challenge the usefulness, it is rather that we think again and put into question the paradigm that the arbitrator, or the three arbitrators, have to do everything themselves and have not to receive assistance. Erik Schäfer, who unfortunately has gone, put a useful point into the discussion. Quality, independence, impartiality, transparency, we have a range of values, and in our debate, especially about secretaries but also other forms of assistance there is — as Zachary Douglas pointed out — a lot of hypocrisy. What is necessary for our discussion here is to look at what type of intervention, what type of assistance we can have and how we can do this in a way that the concerns of the parties are taken care of.

Unfortunately Wolfgang Peter is not here but one of my first experiences when we sat on a tribunal both with a very good secretary but also with a professor from the university in air conditioning, a very complicated subject, and he helped us. We had afterwards a *post mortem* where we got counsel there and asked them: what was your reaction as counsel. They said we were a bit wary but we had confidence in the arbitrators that they would not misuse it and they could come back if new ideas come up in this process. It is something we are losing in the over-formalisation. We are losing the element of confidence in this relationship and in the competence.

I think one other point which was very useful from Zachary Douglas is this question of putting it up-front and saying openly the tribunal needs either a secretary who writes the English better than the tribunal members or an expert. Piero Bernardini is not here anymore but I sat on a tribunal with him where we had three naval architects helping the tribunal getting it right for a very complicated offshore installation. Again, it is a question of transparency.

If you take the message of Professor Pierre Tercier of looking not only at the form but the substantive contributions that can be made and combine it with all the other messages of transparency and independence I think we have made some progress in improving the quality of the process and the comfort which parties have with it. Thank you very much.

Further Written Contributions on the Conference Topic

An Essay on the Challenges to Collegiality

William G. Bassler

When I left the bench in 2006 after sixteen years as a trial judge of the United States District Court, I recognized that arbitration is not litigation and so I took advantage of the excellent educational programs and conferences offered by the institutional providers I was associated with. I also immersed myself in the extensive literature on mediation and arbitration.

Initially, I served most of the time as a sole arbitrator. But as time went by, the amounts in controversy increased and the issues became more complex, and I found myself serving more on panels as chair or wing arbitrator. It was then that I realized that my experience as a trial judge and the educational programs I attended had not fully prepared me for the challenges unique to working with two other arbitrators, who I usually did not know very well, if at all.

What was missing in my experience and education was any discussion, let alone recognition, of the difficulties of working with two other individuals. For example, the *Protocols for Expeditious, Cost-Effective Commercial Arbitrations* published by the College of Commercial Arbitrators focuses on the responsibility of the arbitrators to actively manage and shape the arbitration process, to enforce contractual deadlines and timetables, to clarify the issues, to streamline exchange of information, to discourage filing of unproductive motions, to be readily available to counsel and to conduct fair but expeditions hearings. No mention is made of the responsibility of the arbitrators to each other and to the process. While it is common in the United States for faculty handbooks to state that professional competence includes demonstrated professional and ethical relationships with colleagues, the American Arbitration Association's *Code of Ethics for Arbitrators in Commercial Disputes* makes no mention of collegiality in any of its Canons. It is a subject, I suspect, that is not talked about for fear of breaching confidentiality and impairing relationships.

But the responsibility of arbitrators to each other, which is captured in the word collegiality, is critical to a smooth running and effective arbitration. It is worth remembering that the word collegiality has its root in the Latin word—*collegium*—that is partnership or association. It identifies the relationship that should exist between partners in office who relate to each other in a shared responsibility. It is something more than politeness, which the French philosopher Andre Comte Sponville in his book *A Small Treatise on the Great Virtues* calls "the first virtue, and the origin perhaps of all the others," but nevertheless "a virtue of pure form, of etiquette and ceremony!"

Collegiality certainly encompasses politeness and respect. Like civility in litigation it helps to lubricate the process of contending with conflicting positions and abrasive personalities. And while it is certainly a virtue for arbitrators it is more than "a virtue of pure form, of etiquette and ceremony."

Collegiality is significantly more important than politeness because its absence can seriously impair an arbitrator's performance and the work of the arbitral panel. Collegiality recognizes the obligation of each arbitrator to contribute to the goal of a fair but expeditious hearing.

Let me say that in my limited experience as an arbitrator I have been fortunate in working with arbitrators of the highest integrity and ability. The examples of lack of collegiality that I am about to discuss should be distinguished from flagrant ethical violations. Fortunately, I have not experienced those. I never experienced an environment where one of the arbitrators engaged in ex parte communications with one of the parties, or deliberately tried to sabotage the arbitration. I never had to deal with the situation Serge Lazareff described to me where a party was arranging for female companionship for one of the arbitrators during the arbitration.

My experiences of lack of collegiality are few in number and rather mundane but perhaps you might recognize these challenges to collegiality. Behaviour doesn't have to be criminal to be obnoxious.

In my first international arbitration, every morning one of the arbitrators continuously arrived fifteen to twenty minutes late. There we were with a room full of highly paid lawyers, even higher paid business executives and witnesses anxious to be getting along with their lives and this arbitrator would show up with no apology or explanation. I was not the chair and frankly somewhat intimidated by the arbitrator's current and previous professional standing. I was unsure of what to do. But I can tell you, I was acutely embarrassed. I was afraid that if I confronted him with his continual tardiness and lack of consideration to the panel and the lawyers and the parties that it would poison our relationship and ability to collaborate on the difficult work that lay ahead. Over the years, I have learned the hard way that criticism is not only a waste of time but a source of bitter resentment.

What I did do was to make sure that I got to the hearing early, so that when he arrived the Chair and I would be in our places with everyone in theirs. Eventually the late arriving arbitrator got the message and began arriving on time. Much later after the arbitration was finalized I ran into one of the attorneys at an event outside of London who expressed to me his outrage and his determination never to hire that arbitrator again.

Collegial trespasses should be distinguished from principled positions. I once shared an arbitration with an arbitrator who adamantly refused to discuss anything about the arbitration before deliberations. While I respected his position, I questioned to myself its validity. When I was on the bench, it was customary to instruct the jury not to discuss the evidence before instructions on the law and before formal jury deliberations. The fear was that a juror would take a position in the early discussions that invested that juror with a position that had to be defended, thus preventing the juror from objectively evaluating the evidence. Today I believe that that instruction is not necessarily given and that it is understood by thoughtful judges that discussing the evidence as it come in improves the quality of the decision-making process. The point of my mentioning this arbitrator is not the arbitrator's refusal to discuss the case before deliberations, but his refusal to assist the Chair in drafting the Award. It was a very difficult case with the law of several jurisdictions applying to different documents in the transaction along with complicated facts and challenging credibility determinations. Criticizing his lack of involvement would have been futile, so I simply redoubled my efforts to assist the Chair in editing, checking the facts, and confirming the law.

Arbitrators who are late and arbitrators who are lazy put an unnecessary strain on the process. But more burdensome is the arbitrator who won't listen. I don't mean an arbitrator who won't agree. The virtue of collegiality is not more important than the duty of independence. Collegiality demands that each arbitrator respect the other arbitrator's view of the facts and the law. The facts are often nebulous and the law often equivocal or non-existent. What I am talking about is the arbitrator who is too lazy to review the record or to take the time to study the law or when that has been done too intransigent to even consider revaluation of his or her position. The scenario I am describing presents a tough challenge. It is of course always possible that you may be wrong. But what I am trying to describe is the situation where you are convinced that any objective and careful reading of the law leads to the conclusion you reached.

I am mindful of one of Benjamin Franklin's famous aphorisms that "A Man convinced against his will is of the same opinion still." Your only hope can be that if your analysis is correct, it will find confirmation by the other arbitrator. What I do here is to be as careful and lucid as I can be in explaining my position and hope that the third arbitrator can overcome the "invincible ignorance" of my colleague. I avoid acrimony and critical comment.

In this short essay, I have limited my remarks to several problems that I have encountered. You have undoubtedly confronted these and others. Anything that a colleague does that diverts the Panel's attention to the task at hand and doesn't contribute to collaborative decision making can be a challenge to collegiality. Collegiality is critically important because it vitally affects the performance of arbitrators and enhances the relationships among themselves, counsel and the parties. I recognize that collegiality is not an end in itself, that it doesn't trump the obligation to fairly and impartially resolve the parties' dispute. But it is of great importance in creating an atmosphere where objective decision making can more easily be accomplished. When faced with a challenge to collegiality the approach to take is the one that advances the arbitration. The critical question when faced with a challenge to collegiality is to ask whether your response will hinder or help the deliberative process of reaching the goal of a sound award that you are pleased and proud to sign.

Six Modest Proposals before You Get to the Award

Nicolas Ulmer

Introduction

Most of the emphasis and discussion goes to the arbitrators' post-hearing deliberations and the drafting of the Award. But in a well-organized and structured arbitration the basis of the deliberation, and the discipline needed to reach a correct and timely award, should be planned early on.

In answer to Michael E. Schneider's invitation I offer six modest "logistical" suggestions together with some anecdotal explanation of the discipline required. None of the suggestions are profound, but all are practical — if not always followed.

1. Identify the Points to Proven (and Issues of Law) as Early as Possible

I do not mean merely listing the issues to be resolved as one does in ICC Terms of Reference. I mean an actual discussion with and between parties' counsel and co-arbitrators about what proof and law are envisioned. When possible I ask counsel to be prepared at the first procedural meeting or conference call with a "no prejudice" but intelligent view of the substance of their case/defence. Counsel are sometimes uncomfortable with this — and tentative — but it is still worthwhile. The arbitrator(s) also need to be prepared to give intelligent — if sometimes tentative — instructions and repartee (e.g. "well if that is going to be your position we will need detailed information and pleading on the mandatory corporate law provisions of X" or "we will likely need considerable background on the customs and practices of widget trading"). This focuses matters on what needs to be proved/proffered rather than who is "right" — it also sometimes smokes out an arbitrator whose views may be formed faster than the evidence allows.

Bottom line: Not only procedure, but law and substance should be considered early on.

2. A Proper Pre-Hearing Meeting of Arbitrators

Cohesiveness and thoroughness in the Tribunal are enhanced if they take the time to have a proper pre-hearing meeting to discuss the evidence and issues, and what they are expecting from the hearing (the scheduling of such a formal meeting also heightens the likelihood that the arbitrators will usefully read the file in order to be prepared for the discussion). All too often one or more arbitrator flies in the morning of the arbitration itself, or late the previous night. I recently had an experience as chairman where, appointed by an arbitral institution, I knew neither of the co-arbitrators. I arranged to have a several hour meeting and *then* dinner and drinks. In this case it was also agreed that one of the arbitrators, who had expertise in a particular and pertinent issue of German law would provide a neutral memo to the Tribunal with the latest cases and doctrine. By agreement, I ended up drafting the Award and circulating it and our "deliberations" were efficiently carried out by conference call. I do not believe it would have gone as smoothly if the prior efforts at collegiality had not been undertaken.

Bottom line: Find the time to have a proper pre-hearing meeting.

3. Paying Attention at the Hearing

This injunction to arbitrators would seem self-evident, but it is not always respected. I was Claimant's counsel in an ICC arbitration where all three of the arbitrators were often (almost constantly) sending and receiving messages on their Blackberries *during* witness testimony (they sought to conceal this by holding the devices under the table — but it was still visible and from where my paralegal sat he had a good view of all three, which he reported to me). That same case was a model for two other problems that should be of concern. First, literally 90% of the Chairman's comments concerned speeding up the proceedings, cutting-off areas of testimony, dispensing with the last afternoon of the hearing, so he could get an earlier plane, no translation of the testimony, etc.; in short, the Chairman could not have made more obvious that his priority was to get out of town (Geneva) to return to his office (elsewhere in Europe) and that he had larger cases (this case involved about Euro 15 million in dispute). I should mention that this Chairman is a *very* well-known arbitrator who runs an "arbitration shop". As I have commented elsewhere the "professional arbitrator/arbitration industry" phenomenon is an issue and can interfere with a case being handled properly. I would never agree to this arbitrator again, although he is a "big name", and I am on good terms with him personally (and served with him on a panel — but the case settled early). The other problem in that case was language; one of the arbitrators, it developed, was clearly not fully at home in the language of the arbitration (French). He was selected in large part because he was a prominent lawyer in the country whose substantive law applied to the dispute. The fact that he had to concentrate hard to follow the hearing added to his inattention and, not surprisingly, he never asked a question (but I did notice the difference in his level of attention when a witness testified in his native language). There are many other anecdotes that most experienced arbitration counsel could contribute (the elegant Belgian Chairman who constantly had his secretary come into the hearing room with unrelated letters and documents for him to sign comes to mind), but the point is the same: some arbitrators do not give the hearings their best attention, including many of the "big" busy ones.

Bottom line: Arbitrators should be completely concentrated on the hearing during the hearing, and the case and Award will suffer if they are not.

4. Use the Breaks in the Hearing to Consider Evidence and Build Consensus

No sooner is a break called in a hearing than the arbitrators are on their phones to their offices, or are sending emails. Some of this is inevitable, but it should not be *every* break. Arbitral Tribunals should seize mid-hearing occasions to discuss the evidence they have just heard while it is fresh in their minds. Interestingly I have not infrequently found that not all arbitrators understood the witness the same way—raising issues for possible follow-up in the hearing or on the transcript. It can also be important to use the breaks to discuss what is expected of upcoming witnesses and interrogations the Tribunal may have, i.e. to "take the temperature of the hearing". I remember several arbitrations where one arbitrator was *never* present during the breaks and often had to be located when hearings recommenced. When I am a sole arbitrator, I try to use the break to reread the witness statements of the next witness.

Bottom line: If you leave consideration and discussion of the evidence until the end, it will be too little too late—and the Award will suffer.

5. Reserve Time for Discussion at the End of the Hearing

I remember a fairly large arbitration venued in Miami where the Chairman almost immediately after the hearings caught a plane home. My co-arbitrator and I lived much further away (South-America and Europe) and had to wait until the evening of the next day to get a flight. We tried to make progress on the case, but it was difficult without the Chairman. Moreover, although my co-arbitrator and I got along well we did not agree on one—quite difficult—issue of interpretation (in fact I ended up being a part of the majority and the South-American arbitrator dissented—albeit on that point only not on the other parts of the Award). In another case I made a point of staying an extra day in the distant Latin American capital after the hearing so we could deliberate—as after that all communications would be by email and phone. Unfortunately, despite the Chairman's best efforts, the discussion was unfocussed and my co-arbitrator was far more interested in topping off the hearings with a pleasant lunch (we were able to put that off until 14:00) than in systematic review of the evidence. This same co-arbitrator—although he agreed at the time that the Chairman should circulate a draft—professed to be shocked when he got it. After many long and painful email and phone exchanges this co-arbitrator issued a detailed dissent (whose provenance I would question). While I doubt that any amount of deliberations would have caused this particular arbitrator to see the contract and the evidence the way the Chairman and I did (and we two had very similar views) a longer and more disciplined deliberation would have helped "flush out" the arbitrator's viewpoint (or bias) earlier and reduced this arbitrator's later stated position that his views were not taken into account. If all the arbitrators live in the same area, then this post-hearing deliberation can be put-off—but that is most often not the case, and I have sat on several Tribunals where the three arbitrators lived on different continents many thousands of kilometres and many times zones, apart. In such circumstances it is irresponsible to leave the hearing without seeking a disciplined meeting to discuss evidence and award. The time used for this purpose will almost always result in a better and faster award.

Bottom line: The Tribunal has to seize the time for face to face deliberations before they separate—the failure to do so can be costly.

6. Do Not Delay Writing the Award

All too often an arbitral tribunal, or a sole arbitrator, has blocked out time for the hearing but is then immediately occupied with other cases or matters that have been put off by the hearing. (In one large construction case, a very well-known Chairman had scheduled a month long second honeymoon—I wrote the sections of the Award I had been assigned, but they sat in his box). The result is that it takes weeks, or even months, before the arbitrator turns to the details of the case—which he or she then has to "relearn". In particular (and I know from frustrating personal experience) the arbitrator has lost familiarity with the documents and where to find them. Obviously the process (and it is a process) of writing an arbitral award takes time and reflection (and for the conscientious arbitrator is usually stressful—for the arbitrator the real stress comes at the end). But there is little or no question that better Awards—that are more faithful to and correctly cite evidence—are issued if the process is begun promptly after the close of the evidentiary hearing. If possible it is highly useful for the arbitrator to organize and review the file *before* receiving the Post-Hearing Brief, and not just rely on those briefs to organize evidence. All too often, however, arbitrators are immersed in a wholly different matter once the hearings terminate.

Bottom line: Setting aside the post-hearing time promptly to write the Award pays off in accuracy and quality as well as celerity.

A Short Note on the Decision-making Process

Michael Black

I have been asked to prepare a short note sharing my experiences of the decision-making process within arbitral tribunals. In particular, having expressed some attraction for the allocation of specific tasks to members of the tribunal at the recent ASA/DIS Arbitration Practice Seminar at Badenweiler, and that suggestion having been greeted with a degree of scepticism as to the utility of such a procedure, especially under institutional procedures that assess fees on an *ad valorem* basis, I have been asked in particular how the tasks may be allocated to individual tribunal members and how this affects the allocation of fees.

A point well made at Badenweiler was that the process of dividing up the issues between the arbitrators really only works where there is a homogeneity of legal culture. My experience has only been of tribunals whose members may not originate from the same jurisdictions, but are nevertheless lawyers experienced in the practice of international arbitration. I therefore accept that where tribunal members do not share a legal culture or the collegiality of the international arbitration community, difficulties may arise—*a fortiori* if a party-appointed arbitrator (for whatever reason) closely identifies with the appointing party.

With that caveat, I have found that the procedure works well in matters which involve multiple discrete issues. The Presiding Arbitrator determines the allocation between the members of the tribunal. It is important that the Presiding Arbitrator maintains overall editorial control in order to ensure consistency in the use of terms and in style. Each arbitrator prepares and circulates the relevant section or sections of the award. Each arbitrator then comments on the drafts prepared by the other arbitrators. This often obviates the necessity for lengthy, or even any, deliberation-meetings following the hearing — which can be a cause of delay and expense. It is however important that the arbitrators have the opportunity to meet immediately after the hearing to exchange some preliminary views and discuss the division of labour.

I have not encountered problems in relation to fees. I do admit to a personal preference for hourly rates as the *ad valorem* basis can mean that arbitrators may be seriously under or over-remunerated. I know that the primary justification for the use of the *ad valorem* method of calculation of fees is that it provides a measure of certainty for the parties. It is my experience that the certainty may be more apparent than real as parties (frequently because of protracted interlocutory proceedings) find themselves facing increasing demands for further advances on costs. Hourly rates allow each arbitrator to be remunerated for, and only for, work actually undertaken. However, even under *ad valorem* procedures, I have found that busy international arbitrators are happy to ensure that the members of the tribunal who have borne the greater burden of preparation of the award receive the appropriate proportion of the fees.

Perhaps I have simply been fortunate in my colleagues.

Personal Views on How Arbitral Tribunals Operate and Reach Their Decisions

Nael G. Bunni

In International arbitration, there are more often than not three arbitrators of different nationalities, cultures, education and background. In most cases and under most arbitration rules, it is the duty of the arbitral tribunal, and in the first place its chairman, to prepare a case management scheme for the conduct of the arbitration on which the tribunal is appointed. In my view, case management should involve as a starting point a face to face preliminary meeting with the parties very soon after receiving the case file. At this gathering, besides meeting the parties, the arbitrators would have the first real opportunity to discuss with each other the issues facing them in detail. Extracting those issues at an early stage is the primary task of the tribunal and in this connection I would say the first step to deliberation session between the arbitrators may take place. Hence, it is extremely important, in my view, to have a face to face preliminary meeting rather than an audio or video conference, particularly if the members of the arbitral tribunal had not previously met. These deliberations would give the chairman a good insight into the stature and metal of the other members of the tribunal.

Whilst it may be too early at the stage of the preliminary meeting to start thinking about the decisions that the arbitrators would have to make in order to resolve the issues between the parties and how they should be decided, it is not too early to plan and pave the way for how to approach these issues and the methodology by which the decisions may be accomplished. So, when should arbitrators start thinking about the actual decisions they have to make and when do their deliberations regarding these decisions, or otherwise, start?

Generally speaking, the arbitrators are required to deliberate by mandatory law; by custom; and by the expectation of the parties. Not to do so, would usually result in non-recognition and annulment of the award. Furthermore, the deliberations of the tribunal are confidential and should not be divulged to the parties or to others.

However, before going any further, it is worthwhile to consider the meaning of "deliberation". What is deliberation? Should deliberation take place at a face-to-face meeting between the arbitrators in the place of arbitration or could it be done by correspondence, or even through telephone discussions? If the deliberations take place through correspondence, how thorough should that correspondence be, particularly if one of the arbitrators takes a different view to the other two? Should the chairman record every decision taken and forward it to the co-arbitrators for approval immediately after such a decision is taken? These questions arise from bitter experiences where surprising events have taken place.

As an example of one of these situations, one of the co-arbitrators in a case where I was the chairman in an international arbitration adopted the position of an additional advocate of the views of his appointing party. The deliberations became extremely difficult and sometimes impossible, and his actions ended in writing a dissenting opinion holding that the discussions that had taken place between the members of the arbitral tribunal were not in fact deliberations and that none was held by the tribunal. The award was not honoured and its recognition and enforcement came ultimately before the courts in Egypt ending fortunately in a very uncomfortable situation for that co-arbitrator. The competent Court held against his contention and stated as follows:[1]

> The phrases that have been used by the Arbitrator who is objecting to the Award on the basis that he was not involved in the Tribunal's deliberations is in fact evidence of his having been involved in those deliberations with the other members of the Tribunal. He has knowledge of the deliberations and it seems he has expressed his views on the law to the Tribunal.[2]

It is worth mentioning in this connection that the arbitration law in various jurisdictions require specific conditions for deliberation. For example in Egypt, under Article 40 of the Egyptian Arbitration Law, the award of an arbitral tribunal composed of more than one arbitrator should be issued by a majority of opinions after deliberations conducted in the manner determined by the arbitral tribunal, unless the parties otherwise agree. The important words here are "after deliberations" as they are capable of different interpretations.[3]

---

[1] Cairo Appeal Court, Decision No. 94, Case No. 37, Commercial, 29th March 2006, relating to CRCICA Case no. 175/2000. It is of note that the Cairo Court of Appeal in reaching its Decision, referred to and relied upon the decision of a French Court in Intelcam v. French Telecom, 16th January 2003, Rev. arb. 2004, pp. 369-389.
[2] The quoted text is the writer's translation from the Arabic text of the judgment.
[3] An important aspect of the Egyptian Arbitration law is the difference between Article 40 of the Egyptian Law and Article 29 of the UNCITRAL Model Law, from which it stems, relating to decision-making by a panel of arbitrators.

In another incident in Egypt, the scene turned out to be rather ugly in a different way through a co-arbitrator resorting to frustrating and delaying techniques by becoming unavailable to attend deliberation and decision making sessions, thus preventing the process of deliberation from taking place. Fortunately, that was in an institutional arbitration where the attempts were capable of being recorded and presented to the administering institution.

Having said that the first deliberation session should take place at the preliminary meeting, the invitation to deliberate and the conduct of the deliberation is the responsibility of the chairman. It is expected that during the arbitration process, and before the hearing, many procedural issues would arise which would need to be discussed by the members of the arbitral tribunal who should deliberate by e-mail exchanging their views, sometimes with the chairman offering the first view and others by the chairman asking the views of the co-arbitrators first. However, if the issue is of serious consequences, then such deliberation might have to take place by telephone and/or at a physical meeting of the tribunal, particularly if the problem is of intricate and complex nature. It is extremely important for the co-arbitrators to express their views and offer their help during these deliberations as such exchanges would develop a useful relationship between the members of the arbitral tribunal. However, it is also important for the chairman to be prepared to accept and adopt a better view than his/her own and forget vanity.

The main deliberations would obviously take place and would be necessary during and most definitely after the hearing. The deliberations during the hearing would take place as the evidence is adduced; and discussions should be held between the arbitrators regarding the matters that need to be ventilated. Deliberations would also take place immediately after the hearing in order to establish the procedure for future deliberations and how they should take place and how to proceed with deciding the substantive issues. This would normally lead to establishing how to prepare the next draft(s) of the award; and later after the post-hearing submissions are received; and how to reach the necessary decisions.

If the tribunal has not established a collegiate working relationship and a way to cooperate,[4] the chairman would have to proceed carefully and formally, particularly if one of the arbitrators chooses to act in an improper manner.

In general terms, how to deliberate will depend on the type of issue facing the Tribunal and on whether there are major differences

---

[4] This problem could be the fault of the chairman or the other members of the tribunal.

between the members of the Tribunal. This is particularly important at the early stages of the arbitration which would normally determine how the relationship between the arbitrators would develop.

Deliberation will in some cases test the ability of the chairman and sometimes exhaust his/her patience. However, whatever happens, the thread between the chairman and the co-arbitrators should not be stretched beyond repair nor cut off completely. In normal happier circumstances, deliberation should generate the appropriate and the most suitable answer to the issue being discussed. Constructive deliberation should work as an interaction between the minds of the arbitrators and result in the most appropriate way forward just like when charged clouds collide producing lightening that could show the way forward in an illuminated manner.

It is essential for a successful deliberation between the members of the arbitral tribunal for the chairman to know and understand the cases pleaded by the Parties. Whilst this is essential for the chairman, it is sometimes not easy to ensure that the co-arbitrators are so well prepared. In many instances, co-arbitrators arrive to the hearing with no files and having done little or no preparation of reading the case files.

If the chairman's view is shared by one of the two co-arbitrators, a majority award can then be issued, but if there is no consensus on a particular solution, then the arbitration rules used will have a major influence on how the award will be shaped. Under the ICC Rules, it is the Chairman's position that will prevail whereas under the Rules of the Cairo Regional Centre for International Commercial Arbitration, the Chairman will have to rally with him one of the other arbitrators since a majority award is a necessity. This is a very unpleasant situation to be in for the whole case.

Depending on the circumstances of the case; the quality of the co-arbitrators; the issues encountered; the extent of trust held by the chairman towards his two co-arbitrators; and the degree of cooperation between the members of the arbitral tribunal, the first draft of the whole award should be prepared by the chairman. However, in all cases, it would be of great benefit if the chairman prepares the first draft of the structure of the award and the factual chapters that relate to the factual elements of the case, taking care of the requirements of the applicable arbitration law and other legal provisions:[5]

---

[5] An example of such requirements is Article 203 of the law of Arbitration in Dubai, which stipulates that "the subject of the dispute must be specified in the arbitration deed ..."; or Article 208.3 of that law that requires in a case of more than a sole arbitrator that "... they must jointly carry out the investigation procedures and each must sign the minutes."; or Article 212.4 of that law which requires that "... the award must be issued

- background and essential details of the Contract in question, including the arbitration clause or agreement;
- the appointment of the tribunal;
- the preliminary meeting and the steps taken to agree on a provisional timetable;
- the procedure adopted and the procedural orders rendered;
- the submissions of the Parties leading to the hearing; and
- all the other factual matters that took place prior to the hearing,

and present that draft to the other members of the tribunal at the commencement of the hearing for the start of their deliberations.

Besides the fact that such a discipline would allow the chairman to be up to date with the progress of the case, it is helpful to present to the co-arbitrators that draft before the hearing which would help to identify the questions that need to be investigated and dealt with during the hearing. However, it is imperative in my view for the chairman to refrain from setting down any pre-conceived views on the basis of preliminary thinking of how the issues in the case might be resolved or decided. It is therefore important for the chairman to simply set down in this first draft of the award the factual parts of the award without any analysis of the issues involved.

Of course, it is always the preference to have a unanimous award, which requires much patience and hard work, but if this proves to be impossible, then a majority award will have to do provided that all the members of the arbitral tribunal are independent, impartial and neutral with views that are honestly held. Whilst it is expected that a co-arbitrator would endeavour to have the contentions of the party that appointed him/her properly aired and considered during the proceedings, it is not permissible for the co-arbitrator to act as an advocate, since to do so would discredit the whole process.

---

in the United Arab Emirates; ..."; or Article 212.5 of that law which requires that the award "... must be written along with the dissenting opinion and must specifically include a copy of the arbitration agreement, ..."; or Article 216.a requiring a valid arbitration deed, etc.

Notes and Samples on Tribunal Deliberations

Karl-Heinz Böckstiegel

At the request of ASA, as I am unable to attend the ASA-Conference in Zurich on 1 February 2013, *Inside the Black Box: How Arbitral Tribunals Operate and Reach their Decisions*, it is with pleasure that I submit a few notes and samples on the topic of the meeting.

1. Extract from Address "Party Autonomy and Case Management – 40 Years of Arbitral Experience" at the DIS Conference "Organising Arbitral Proceedings – Regulations, Options and Recommendations" in Berlin 24/25 October 2012:

    Deliberations and Decisions by the Tribunal

    Finally, the planning and conduct of the deliberations by the tribunal after the hearing till the issuance of an award should also be part of case management.

    As we know, it is often claimed that today arbitrations take too long. I agree, but must add from my own experience, that the length is mostly due to the fact that, as mentioned earlier, parties and their counsel request and indeed often need long periods to elaborate and submit their submissions and evidence.

    However, I also see that some tribunals, after the hearing and closure of the procedure take astonishingly long periods of time until their award is issued. This may be partly due to some arbitrators accepting too many appointments, or to strong dissents between the members of the tribunal which cannot be resolved shortly, or simply that some are badly organized.

    As some in this room know from joining me on tribunals, I try to start early in the procedure the elaboration of what I call the Tribunal Working Paper (TWP) which summarizes the major procedural and substantive aspects of the case and contentions of the parties, of course without any pre-judgement. This TWP is distributed to my Co-Arbitrators and regularly updated as the procedure goes on, at the latest right after the hearing and possible Post Hearing Briefs. It then provides the starting point for well-informed deliberations of the Tribunal and usually allows a speedy process until the

Award. But of course, depending on the complexity of the case and possible dissents in the tribunal, it may still not always be possible to issue the award very shortly.

2. Sample Outline of Tribunal Working Paper (TWP)

The following is a sample of a TWP from an LCIA arbitration in which the identification of the Case, the Parties, the Tribunal, and the Issues have been redacted:

LCIA case………..

TRIBUNAL WORKING PAPER (TWP 3)

PHASE II OF THE PROCEDURE

Date ………..

The Arbitral Tribunal:

……….. (Arbitrator)

……….. (Arbitrator)

……….. (Chairman)

TABLE OF CONTENTS

Abbreviations

A. The Parties and Their Counsel

B The Arbitral Tribunal

C. Short Identification of the Case

    C.I. The Claimant's Perspective

    C.II. The Respondent's Perspective

D. Procedural History

E. Relevant Legal Texts

    E.I. Relevant Provisions of the Agreement

    E.II. Relevant Provisions of the Civil Code

    E.III. Relevant Provisions of the Statute on Joint Stock Companies

F. Relief Sought by the Parties

- F.I. Relief Sought by Claimant
- F.II. Relief Sought by the Respondent
- G. Factual Background
  - G.I. Relevant History of the Parties
  - G.II. Events Leading to the Agreement
  - G.III. The Conclusion of the Agreement
  - G.IV. The disputed AGM
  - G.V. Events Post-Initiation of Arbitration
  - G.VI. Table of Named Persons and Entities
- H. The Disputed Issues
  - H.I. Summary of Contentions by Claimant
  - H.II. Summary of Contentions by Respondent
- J. Preliminary Considerations and Conclusions of the Tribunal
  - J.I. Applicable Law
  - J.II. Jurisdiction
- K. Considerations and Conclusions of the Tribunal Regarding Liability on Claims
  - K.I. Whether the Initial Transfer Involved a Breach of Agreement
    1. Arguments by Claimant
    2. Arguments by Respondent
    3. The Tribunal
  - K.II. Whether the X and Y Transactions Involved a Breach of the Agreement
    1. Arguments by Claimant
    2. Arguments by Respondent
    3. The Tribunal
  - K.III. Did the Breach of Art. ... Cause the Failure of the Memorandum
    1. Arguments by Claimant

- 2. Arguments by Respondent
- 3. The Tribunal

K.IV. Did Respondent Breach the Agreement with Respect to the Memorandum
- 1. Arguments by Claimant
- 2. Arguments by Respondent
- 3. The Tribunal

K.V. Whether Respondent is Guilty of Tortious Conspiracy
- 1. Arguments by Claimant
- 2. Arguments by Respondent
- 3. The Tribunal

L. Considerations and Conclusions of the Tribunal Regarding Quantum on Claims

L.I. Summary of Arguments Relating to Quantum

L.II. Whether Damages Resulted to Claimant as a Result of the Initial Transfer
- 1. Arguments by Claimant
- 2. Arguments by Respondent
- 3. The Tribunal

L.III. Damages Resulting from the X and Y Transactions
- 1. Arguments by Claimant
- 2. Arguments by Respondent
- 3. The Tribunal

L.IV. Damages Arising from the Breach of the Agreement at the AGM
- 1. Arguments by Claimant
- 2. Arguments by Respondent
- 3. The Tribunal

L.V. Damages Arising from a Breach of the Agreement with respect to the Memorandum
- 1. Arguments by Claimant

NOTES AND SAMPLES ON TRIBUNAL DELIBERATIONS 133

        2. Arguments by Respondent

        3. The Tribunal

    L.VI. Damages Arising from a Tortious Conspiracy

        1. Arguments by Claimant

        2. Arguments by Respondent

        3. The Tribunal

    L.VII The Claim for an Account of Profits

        1. Arguments by Claimant

        2. Arguments by Respondent

        3. The Tribunal

M. Defences to Quantum Claims

    M.I Defence of Reflective Loss

        1. Arguments by Respondent

        2. Arguments by Claimant

        3. The Tribunal

    M.II. The Duty to Mitigate Damages

        1. Arguments by Respondent

        2. Arguments by Claimant

        3. The Tribunal

N. Considerations and Conclusions of the Tribunal Regarding the Counter Claims

    N.I Summary of Arguments Regarding Counter Claims

    N.II Counter Claim for $400 million

        1. Arguments by Respondent (Counter-Claimant)

        2. Arguments by Claimant (Counter-Respondent)

        3. The Tribunal

    N.III Respondent's Entitlement to Same Style of Damages as Claimed by Claimant

        1. Arguments by Respondent (Counter-Claimant)

    2. Arguments by Claimant (Counter-Respondent)
    3. The Tribunal
O. Interest
  O.I. Arguments by Claimant
  O.II. Arguments by Respondent
  O.III. The Tribunal
P. Arbitration Costs
  P.I. Arguments by Claimant
  P.II. Arguments by Respondent
  P.III. The Tribunal

Arbitration Materials

Example of Decision Tree

Introduction

The case was mainly about an early termination of a long term supply contract whereby the question of whether or not the early termination was valid/invalid played a major role. The other questions were somewhat subsidiary to this principal decision and it was obvious that the Arbitral Tribunal will be split over the termination issue (as the parties were). There were procedural issues as well, over which the par- ties carried out bitter disputes.

The applicable law was from a Southern European (civil law) country, other than Switzerland. All parties, party representatives and all arbitrators, except for the Swiss Chairman, were from that Southern European Country (hereinafter referred to as "XY").

The decision tree was meant and did serve the Arbitrators to (1) define their respective positions on the many issues internally and (2) thereafter to "negotiate" solutions on the overall issues. The outcome was a unanimous decision in the end.

ICC Case No. XXXX (1998 Rules)

ICC Award Decision Tree

I. Jurisdiction, Place of Arbitration and Applicable Law

- Jurisdiction: not in dispute—ICC Court of Arbitration (Art. 16 of Agreement)

- Place of Arbitration: no longer in dispute—Zurich (party agreement in ToR)

- Applicable Law: not in dispute—XY law applicable (Art. 16 of Agreement)

II. Legal Analysis/Decisions to be taken

    A. Procedural Issues

        1. Did Claimant's change of its original compensation claim (RfA) to a performance claim (SoC)?

            Considerations and decision of Arbitral Tribunal: _____

2. If yes, was this allowed under Art. 19 ICC Rules?

   Considerations and decision of Arbitral Tribunal: _____

3. Any consequences?

   Considerations and decision of Arbitral Tribunal: _____

B. Substantive Issues

1. Has a valid Supply Agreement (SA) been concluded?
   not in dispute

2. Who were the parties to the SA and what were their main contractual duties?
   not in dispute

3. Termination (heavily in dispute)

   3.1 Ordinary termination (Art. 14 SA)

   3.1.1 Term

   "shall terminate upon completion of the supply of [Contract]-Volume…"

   3.1.2 Ordinary termination

   "if the other party is in material breach … and has not remedied such breach within thirty (30) days…"

   3.1.3 No ordinary termination

   not in dispute that there was no ordinary termination under Art. 14

   3.2 Extraordinary termination (under XY law)

   3.2.1 Termination for serious cause (Answer to RfA, item 10.1) ?

   a) Is SA to be qualified as standing or non-standing contract?

   Significance: Claimant alleges (and the XY arbitrators agree) that under XY law only **standing** [continuous] contracts can be terminated for serious cause, but not **non-standing** [fixed term] contracts with successive partial performances. Claimant considers SA to be a non-standing [fixed term] contract.

Considerations and decision of Arbitral Tribunal: _____

b) If the SA is to be qualified as non-standing [fixed term] contract, is termination for serious cause possible?

Considerations and decision of Arbitral Tribunal: _____

c) If SA is to be qualified as a standing agreement, were there sufficient *serious grounds* to terminate it?

By letter dated [...], the SA was unilaterally terminated by Respondent, based on (alleged) essential changes of the "scientific and factual data" upon which the Agreement was concluded. Respondent maintains that "the continuation of (the) contractual relation could no longer be requested from XYZ [Respondent], as the contractual relation had become excessively burdensome for XYZ" (RfA, No. 14, Exh. C-6).

In the arbitration briefs, additional grounds were relied upon by Respondent to justify the termination:

(it follows a long list of changed circumstances);

Considerations and decision of Arbitral Tribunal: _____

3.2.2 Termination under Art. 288 XY Civil Code?

Same grounds invoked as under 3.2.1.

Are the conditions for application of Art. 288 XY Civil Code met?

Considerations and decision of Arbitral Tribunal: _____

3.2.3 Termination under Art. 388 XY Civil Code?

Same grounds invoked as under 3.2.1.

Are the conditions for application of Art. 388 XY Civil Code met?

Considerations and decision of Arbitral Tribunal: _____

3.3 In all of the above extraordinary terminations, can the termination be invoked by an extrajudicial declaration, or only in a court proceeding (as alleged by Claimant)?

Considerations and decision of Arbitral Tribunal: _____

3.4 Other relevant considerations in connection with termination, if any

Considerations and decision of Arbitral Tribunal: _____

3.5 Conclusion on termination:

Is Respondent's termination valid or not valid?

Considerations and decision of Arbitral Tribunal: _____

C. Alternative 1: If termination by Respondent is considered to be valid by AT

Principal rule: Claimant no longer may deliver, Respondent no longer needs to pay.

Exception to this rule: Shall/can the Arbitral Tribunal simply adapt the obligations of both parties to the new circumstances instead of honouring the termination?

1. Shall there be a total dismissal of the claim, or only an adaptation?

   Considerations and decision of Arbitral Tribunal: _____

2. If an adaption is possible and appropriate, what is the fair solution?

   Considerations and decision of Arbitral Tribunal: _____

3. As of which date is a termination/adaptation effective?

   Ex nunc (from decision onwards, as Claimant maintains) or *ex tunc* (with retroactive effect, as Respondent maintains)

   Considerations and decision of Arbitral Tribunal: _____

4. Any other consequences?

   Can Claimant request negative interest (compensation of production costs for unused [products], or compensation of any other losses?

   Considerations and decision of Arbitral Tribunal: _____

   If such negative interest may be requested, is it proven and in what amount?

   Considerations and decision of Arbitral Tribunal: _____

D. Alternative 2: If termination of Respondent is considered to be invalid

   1. Mutual Claims for Performance

      Principal rule: *pacta sunt servanda*. Claimant is obliged to deliver the goods, Respondent is obliged to take delivery and to pay for the goods. Since the contract is a bilateral one, the Claimant's own performance is a pre-condition for seeking Respondent's payments, or for requesting damages.

      Exceptions to this rule?

      Is Claimant released from its delivery duty, because of Respondent's behaviour?

      Is Respondent released from its payment duty, because of Claimant's behaviour?

      1.1 Is Claimant released from performing (making deliveries) due to Respondent's behaviour (creditor's default Arts 349-358 XY Civil Code)?

         1.1.1 Respondent's explicit refusal to accept deliveries?

            Considerations and decision of Arbitral Tribunal: _____

         1.1.2 Respondent's failure to pick-up goods at Claimant's factory (did SA contain an *ex works* clause? If yes, significance?)

            Considerations and decision of Arbitral Tribunal: _____

- 1.1.3 Did Respondent's behaviour result in the expiration of the [products] and thus made performance by Claimant impossible?

  Considerations and decision of Arbitral Tribunal: _____

- 1.1.4 Other alleged defaults by Respondent. Namely?

  Considerations and decision of Arbitral Tribunal: _____

- 1.1.5 Conclusions as to Respondent's performance obligations (was there creditor's default)?

  Considerations and decision of Arbitral Tribunal: _____

1.2 Is Respondent released from performing (duty to pay) as of 30 December 2009, due to Claimant's behaviour?

- 1.2.1 Was there a duty/lack of Claimant to set a deadline for Respondent's performance?

  Considerations and decision of Arbitral Tribunal: _____

- 1.2.2 Was there a duty/lack of Claimant to sufficiently tender (offer) or place at the disposal of Respondent the goods after 30 December 2009?

  What is needed on the part of Claimant? Verbal offer/written offer/deposit in a warehouse?

  Considerations and decision of Arbitral Tribunal: _____

- 1.2.3 Does it matter that Claimant can no longer fulfil its delivery obligations due to the expiration of the [products]?

  Considerations and decision of Arbitral Tribunal: _____

- 1.2.4 Could/should Claimant have avoided the expiration of [products] by using them for other customers? And, were other customers still available after [date]?

Considerations and decision of Arbitral Tribunal: _____

1.2.5 Were there other deficiencies of Claimant, releasing Respondent from its payment obligations? If yes, which ones?

Considerations and decision of Arbitral Tribunal: _____

1.2.6 Conclusions as to Claimant's performance obligation

Considerations and decision of Arbitral Tribunal: _____

1.3 Overall conclusions as to the Parties' mutual performance claims

Considerations and decision of Arbitral Tribunal: _____

2. Claims for Compensation

If termination is not valid and Respondent is not released from performing, but performance is no longer possible due to the circumstances, then the principal rule is: Respondent is liable for all of Claimant's loss or damage. Claimant has the burden of proof for its damage.

Exception to this rule: If Claimant contributed to the damage, or failed to mitigate it, appropriate damage deductions need to be made.

2.1 What damage has occurred and is proven?

2.1.1 Has Claimant produced/purchased the remaining [products]?

Is it relevant that ABC-A [an Affiliate of ABC] was the actual producer of the [products], and not Claimant ABC?

Considerations and decision of Arbitral Tribunal: _____

Respondent alleges that Claimant lacks "active legitimation" to file the claim as it has not itself produced any [products]

Considerations and decision of Arbitral Tribunal: _____

Respondent alleges that the remaining [products] were no more produced (by any ABC company) after the termination date.

Considerations and decision of Arbitral Tribunal: _____

2.1.2 Is Claimant's calculation of the "gross damage" (€7 per [product]) unit correct and convincing?

Considerations and decision of Arbitral Tribunal: _____

2.1.3 If not, what is the correct calculation of "gross damage"?

Considerations and decision of Arbitral Tribunal: _____

2.2 Did Claimant contribute to, or fail to mitigate, the damage? (Art. 300, 427 and 428 XY Civil Code)?

2.2.1 If there was a damage contribution by Claimant: What is the prejudice imputable to Claimant's fault?

Considerations and decision of Arbitral Tribunal: _____

2.2.2 If there was a failure to mitigate the damage by Claimant: What was the prejudice imputable to Claimant's fault?

Considerations and decision of Arbitral Tribunal: _____

2.2.3 Were there other deficiencies for which Claimant was responsible?

Did Claimant fail by not using the produced [products] for other [products] or different pharmaceutical products (question: was this alleged by Respondent)?

Considerations and decision of Arbitral Tribunal: _____

2.3 Are deductions to be made from Claimant's "gross damage" for Claimant's contribution to, or fail to mitigate, the damage? What is the impact on the damage calculation, i.e. what is the "net damage"?

Considerations and decision of Arbitral Tribunal: _____

E. Conclusions as the Requested Reliefs

1. Are Claimant's Requests for Relief to be granted?

Considerations and decision of Arbitral Tribunal: _____

2. Are Respondent's Requests for Relief to be granted?

Considerations and decision of Arbitral Tribunal: _____

3. Conclusions on quantum

Considerations and decision of Arbitral Tribunal: _____

F. Interest

Claimant asks for "legal interest, calculated from the date of termination of the Agreement. Alternatively, from the date of ABC's [Claimant's] refusal letter to the said termination; again alternatively from the date of submission of the Request for Arbitration". What is correct?

Or is the correct date for interest the date of raising the plea in the Arbitration? Or even a later date, i.e. the Arbitral Tribunal's decision?

Considerations and decision of Arbitral Tribunal: _____

G. Costs

Both parties submitted fees and cost claims. Are they reasonable? Other important points?

Considerations and decision of Arbitral Tribunal: _____

III. Final Award

1.
2.
3.
4.

Example of Dissenting Opinion in an Award

Extract from an Award: place of arbitration Lisbon, 2003

ICC Case N° 00000 (XXX v. ZZZ)

DISSENTING OPINION

Arbitrator

The case to which the present opinion relates is difficult, in particular because of the very complex technical and legal issues which raises, the enormous size of the File, both with respect to the evidence and the Parties' written and oral argument, and the antagonistic spirit in which it was argued by the Parties.

Addressing this case and preparing the Award required great efforts of all members of the Tribunal, in particular of its Chairman. I wish to stress that the work of the Tribunal was characterised by perfect impartiality and a spirit of collegiality under the outstanding direction of its Chairman. This allowed us to reach unanimous conclusions on most of the issues which we had to decide, including the most difficult ones relating to the fitness for purpose of, and the defects in the Works, as well as the remediation that we order the Respondent to perform.

In these circumstances I regret that it was not possible to reach full agreement on all aspects of our Award. The two points on which the members of the Tribunal did not reach unanimity and the grounds on which we disagree, in my view, are such the reasons for this disagreement, as I see them, should be expressed in the present Opinion. These two points relate (1) to the decision concerning liquidated damages and (2) to the authorisation granted to the Respondent to continue withholding outstanding payments.

Example of Dissenting Arbitrator Refusing to Sign the Award

Note at the end of the award, following the signatures of the Chairman and Arbitrator A:

The draft of this award was communicated to Arbitrator B. He was invited to comment at meetings at [the place of arbitration] or in writing. As announced by the Chairman, the other members of the Tribunal travelled to [the place of arbitration] to hear and consider Arbitrator B's comments, if any, at meetings starting on [Day X] and to sign the award. No written objections to the draft were received from Arbitrator B by [Day X]. The [Arbitration Institution] informed the other members of the Tribunal that Arbitrator B did come to the [Institution on Day X] but did not wish to meet them. They therefore concluded that Arbitrator B had no objection to raise against the draft award but that, in line with the position consistently adopted by him with respect to previous partial awards, he did not wish to sign the present final award. Therefore, the Chairman of the Tribunal and Arbitrator A proceeded to sign the award, as it had been previously communicated to Arbitrator B, after having completed the award by entering the amounts of the arbitration costs according to the information provided by the [Arbitration Institution].

Mandate of Tribunal-Appointed Expert on Scheduling

ICC ARBITRATION CASE NO: 00000

MANDATE OF THE ARBITRAL TRIBUNAL'S INDEPENDENT EXPERT ON SCHEDULING

1. The Tribunal's scheduling expert (the "Expert") will generally assist the Tribunal in its review of the Argument and expert evidence tendered by the Parties in respect of schedule delay and the claim for a schedule extension in regard of Change Order xxx. This may include the following tasks:

   (a) reviewing the relevant pleadings, witness statements, exhibits, expert reports submitted and portions of the hearing transcripts to assist the Tribunal in evaluating the scheduling issues before it;

   (b) meeting with the Parties' respective experts who testified in the Change Order xxx proceedings (Messrs. LLL and MMM) to review with them their experts' reports and testimony and to identify those facts and issues on which they agree and clarify and focus the points on which they disagree;

   (c) preparing a report which identifies any areas of agreement and any relevant factual disputes between the Parties' respective experts and which identifies and focusses on the specific scheduling issues for the Tribunal's decision;

   (d) responding to questions the Tribunal has with respect to scheduling issues as they arise in the arbitration; and

   (e) meeting with and generally assisting the Tribunal in understanding and evaluating the expert evidence and scheduling analyses presented to it.

2. The Tribunal does not intend the Tribunal Expert to prepare her own separate scheduling analysis of the scheduling issues between the Parties. However, the Tribunal may ask the Expert to offer an opinion on certain specific issues in dispute between the Parties or on the expert evidence or analyses presented by the Parties.

3. The Tribunal's Expert will be appointed to assist the Tribunal with respect to the scheduling issues arising from Change Order xxx. However, if the Tribunal determines it requires assistance

with the Parties (Change Order yyyy or the zzzz claims), it may also have recourse to the same Expert in regard of these disputes. If the Tribunal does intend to request the assistance of the Expert in this regard, it shall advise the Parties and provide them with an opportunity to present their comments.

4. The materials reviewed by the Expert shall consist only of pleadings, witness statements, expert reports, exhibits in the record and relevant portions of the transcript of the proceedings. No new materials not in the record shall be presented to the Expert during any meeting she may have with the Parties' respective experts.

5. The Tribunal shall provide the Parties with a list of the materials provided to the Expert for her review. The Parties will be entitled to request that other materials forming part of the record be submitted to the Expert. The Tribunal shall decide, in its discretion, whether any such materials should be submitted to the Expert.

6. Any meetings the Expert may have with the Parties' respective experts shall be for the purpose of clarifying the experts' reports and testimony, identifying those facts and issues on which the experts agree and disagree and responding to the Tribunal Expert's questions. No new presentation shall be made nor shall new materials be presented in such meetings. Any meeting between the Tribunal Expert and the Parties' respective experts shall be held in the presence of both such experts. Meetings of the Expert with the Parties' experts may be attended by one member of each Party's counsel team who shall act only as an observer of the meeting and shall not further advocate his or her client's position. Any issues arising at or from any meeting of the experts shall be addressed promptly with the Tribunal and shall not be debated at the experts' meeting.

7. Requests by the Tribunal to the Expert to provide an opinion on the substance of the scheduling issues in dispute between the Parties and any answer or report produced by the Expert shall be made available to the Parties who shall be provided with an opportunity to comment on the report and make submissions to the Tribunal in regard of it. The Tribunal may invite the Parties to provide comments on the questions or topics that it requests the Expert to address.

8. In consultation with the Parties, the Tribunal shall fix an advance to cover the expected fees and expenses of the Tribunal's Expert. The advances shall be paid in equal portions by the Parties and deposited with the ICC Secretariat which shall pay the Expert from time to time upon presentation of invoices in due form supported by appropriate receipts. The fees and expenses of the Expert shall be included in the Tribunal's eventual award on costs.

9. The Expert shall be independent of the Parties and shall disclose any previous dealings with any of the Parties, their principals or counsel for either Party.

10. The Tribunal shall offer the Parties an opportunity to comment on the Expert it selects prior to confirming her appointment.

Tribunal Assistant: Scheduling Expert

Extract from an Award: place of arbitration Cairo, 20 December 2011

Concerning the Programmes Issue, the Parties agreed at the November 2006 hearing that it would be useful for the Tribunal to be assisted by an expert in the field of Programming. They accepted the Tribunal's proposal to appoint **Ms AAA as the Tribunal's Programming Expert (TPE)**. A biographical note on Ms AAA had been distributed to the Parties prior to the Hearing. Ms AAA was informed of her appointment and submitted a quotation for her financial conditions. The Parties considered these conditions and accepted them. Thereupon, Ms AAA was engaged and travelled to Cairo. She attended the Hearing from 28 to 30 November 2006.

With the assistance of the Parties' Programming experts (Mr CCC and Mr CCC), Ms AAA acquainted herself with the relevant elements of the file. She then discussed with the Parties' experts the factual parameters by reference to which the claims for the delay and disruption and the counterclaim for liquidated damages were to be decided.

At the end of the day on 30 November 2006 Ms AAA reported to the Tribunal, in the presence of the Parties and their experts, on the progress achieved in the discussions with the Parties' Programming experts. In particular, she identified where a common understanding had been reached between the experts, identified two critical issues for decision by the Tribunal and described the programme for further work of the Programming experts. A summary of that report, dated 3 December 2006, was delivered to the Parties.

Ms AAA reported on the extent to which the programmes had been identified which served for the Contractor's planning during the performance of the Contract. She explained the progress that had been made in identifying the as-built matrix and announced that completion of this work was expected by early January 2007. As to the Baseline Programme Ms AAA identified the difference between the Parties Programming experts which had to be decided by the Tribunal.

With respect to further work by the experts, Ms AAA explained that the experts intended to apply for the delay analysis a methodology using forward looking time slices, determining for each slice any delayed activities and the amount of delay on them. The experts would then analyse causation and seek to identify the driving factors for the delay. It would then be for the Tribunal to resolve remaining differences, in particular determine the responsibility for the specific delays so identified. The Parties' programming experts agreed that the presentation of Ms AAA fairly represented the conclusions reached in their discussion. It was agreed that the process of identifying and exchanging required documents continue under the direction of Ms AAA who could address herself to the Tribunal in case of any difficulties.

At the November 2006 Hearing the experts concluded that in order to enable them to make further progress in their work, the Tribunal had to decide which baseline had to be used in the delay analysis (**Baseline Issues**). The relevant issues were defined as follows:

[...]

The Tribunal heard argument and received submissions on this issue. It rendered a reasoned decision on the issue in **Procedural Order N° 9** of 10 March 2007.

[...]

The **Time Related (or Delay) Claims**, which are the principal subject of this Final Award, were examined in parallel to the proceedings on the Measurement Claims. For this purpose, the Parties' experts and the Tribunal's Programming Expert had divided the entire period of the works into 18 Time Slices of a duration of three months each (with the exception of the first and the last Time Slice).

For each of these Time Slices the Parties each prepared documents, submissions and reports by their respective programming experts, identifying the delay which, according to them occurred during the Time Slice in question and the causes for such delay. The Tribunal's Programming Expert prepared a report in which she examined these submissions and presented her conclusions. The delay and its causes were then examined at a number of hearings. The method of this examination will be described in further detail below in Chapter 7.

Starting in November 2008 the Parties delivered to the Tribunal in successive stages the Core Files containing the documentary evidence on which they relied for the analysis concerning each of the Time Slices. The production of these core files continued until the May 2009 hearing. The documentary evidence was completed subsequently by documents produced during the hearings.

The delay and its causes then were examined, Time Slice by Time Slice, in a series of hearings starting during the hearing of 23 November to 4 December 2008 and completed at the hearing held from 18 to 22 October 2009. At these hearings the Parties and their experts were given extensive opportunity to present their views and the evidence on which they relied and to respond to the Tribunal's questions. [The Tribunal's Programming Expert attended these hearings and, on occasions, was consulted by the Tribunal, expressing her opinion in front of the Parties and their experts.]

Tribunal Assistant: Scheduling Expert Terms of Reference

Extract from an Award: place of arbitration Cairo, 2011

The Cairo Regional Centre for
International Commercial Arbitration

Case N° 000

DDDD Claimants

v.

FFFF, Respondent

TERMS OF REFERENCE FOR THE

PROGRAMMING EXPERT

ASSISTING THE ARBITRAL TRIBUNAL

1. Under a Contract concluded on xxx, the Parties provided for the construction and equipment by the Claimants of the ... Complex at ...against an agreed contract sum.

2. A dispute has arisen between the Parties with respect to certain claims and was brought before the Cairo Regional Centre for International Commercial Arbitration (the Centre). The case was registered under the Number 0000. An arbitral tribunal was formed which now is composed of CCCC and GGGG Arbitrators, and HHHH, Chairman of the Tribunal.

3. In this dispute, important and complex programming issues are brought before the Tribunal. The Parties agreed with the Tribunal that it would be useful for the Tribunal to be assisted by an expert in the field of programming.

4. Having seen a biographical note showing her qualifications and having been informed about her financial conditions, the Parties agreed that Ms AAAA be appointed as Programming Expert assisting the Arbitral Tribunal.

5. Further to the discussions with the Parties, the Tribunal now confirms as follows the mission of the Tribunal's Programming Expert (the Expert):

    5.1 The Expert shall be at the Tribunal's service in identifying and addressing issues related to programming.

    5.2 For this purpose, she shall have access to all of the Parties submissions, including documentary and witness evidence and the Parties' expert reports.

5.3 The Tribunal's Expert may meet with the Parties' experts, discuss with them their opinion, seeking any clarification which she deems necessary with respect to the opinion and the underlying assumptions. In addition, she shall determine the relevant points on which the Parties' experts agree and those on which they differ and shall attempt to reduce these points of difference.

5.4 When the Tribunal finds this useful, the Expert may meet with the Tribunal for reporting and questioning on the clarification obtained from the Parties' experts. She shall not express an opinion on the soundness or otherwise of the positions taken by the Parties and their experts.

5.5 The Expert shall regularly report on the progress of her work, including any progress on her efforts in reconciling the differences in the positions of Parties' experts. The Parties shall receive copies of these reports and shall be given an opportunity for commenting

5.6 The Tribunal may instruct the Expert to prepare a report setting out her independent expert opinion on any issue of programming. It shall inform the Parties when it gives such instructions and shall afford them an opportunity for commenting the opinion so expressed by the Expert.

6. For the purposes of all communications with the Parties and their experts, the following contact persons have been identified:

For the Claimant:

In respect of the day to day issues concerning the experts and their interaction with the Tribunal's Expert contact shall be Mr NNNN;

in respect of the provision of documents and data held by the Claimant the contact shall be Mr MMMM

For the Respondent:

Mr PPPP

7. In case of any difficulties arising during the course of her consultation with the Parties' experts, the Expert shall contact the Chairman of the Arbitral Tribunal who shall give further directions to the Tribunal's Expert and, if so required by the circumstances, to the Parties and their experts. If the difficulties persist, the Expert shall prepare a note addressed to the Tribunal, describing the incident and indicating any consequences which it may have on the Tribunal's findings. The Parties will be given an opportunity of commenting on such a note and the Tribunal will

give the instructions or summons that it may deem required under the circumstances.

8. The costs and expenses of the Expert are subject to the following modalities:

   8.1 The Experts financial conditions are set out in her letter to the Chairman of the Tribunal dated 25 November 2006. The Parties have paid to the Centre deposits in conformity with these conditions.

   8.2 Any changes to these conditions, in particular any increase in the volume of work requiring additional fees, shall be reported by the Expert to the Tribunal which shall, after consultation of the Parties, make the necessary adjustments. The Parties shall pay in equal shares any additional deposit that may be required.

   8.3 Payments to the Expert shall be made by the Centre against invoices to be verified by the Centre in consultation with the Tribunal. The Parties shall receive copies of the invoices and be informed of such payments.

   8.4 All payments made by the Parties on account of the Expert's services to the Tribunal shall form part of the Costs of the Arbitration to be allocated by a decision of the Arbitral Tribunal.

9. The Expert undertakes to keep strictly confidential her assignment and all documents and information which are made available to her in the course of it. Unless expressly authorised to do otherwise by the Parties or the Tribunal, she may not reveal any of this information to third Parties.

Cairo, ... 2007

The Expert	for the Tribunal
[Signature]	[Signature]
AAAA	HHHHH
	Chairman of the Arbitral Tribunal

The Parties have agreed to the terms of the Expert's mission and accept the present Terms of Reference:

For the Claimants	For the Respondent
[Signature]	[Signature]

Attachment: the Expert's letter of 25 November 2006

Tribunal Assistant: Quantification Expert

Extract from an Award: place of arbitration Cairo, 20 December 2011

In Procedural Order No 12 dated 5 December 2007 the Tribunal also made provision for the quantification of the costs for which the Claimant sought compensation on account of the delay for which it held the Respondent responsible.

The Tribunal heard the Parties on the appointment of **Mr XXX as the Tribunal's Quantification Expert** on 14 April 2008. The Parties had no objections against this appointment. Mr XXX attended some of the hearings and prepared reports which were submitted to the Parties with an opportunity for commenting.

The expert assisted the Tribunal in the calculations. The Parties were informed of advice on the substance of the dispute by Mr XXX and were given an opportunity to comment. As part of this advice Mr XXX prepared a **table of delay costs**, as they were claimed with respect to the different time slices into which the overall construction period had been divided. This table and its content were examined with the Parties' experts. It then served for the calculation of the delay claims, as they are decided in this arbitration. In its final form it forms Attachment B to the present Final Award.

Tribunal Assistant: Quantification Expert Terms of Reference

The Cairo Regional Centre for
International Commercial Arbitration

Case N° 000

AAAA, Claimants

v.

BBBB, Respondent

TERMS OF REFERENCE FOR THE

QUANTIFICATION EXPERT

ASSISTING THE ARBITRAL TRIBUNAL

1. Under a Contract concluded on ..., the Parties provided for the construction and equipment by the Claimants of the ... Complex at ... for an agreed contract sum.

2. A dispute has arisen between the Parties with respect to certain claims and was brought before the Cairo Regional Centre for International Commercial Arbitration (the Centre). The case was registered under the Number 0000. An arbitral tribunal was formed which now is composed of DDDD, EEEE, Arbitrators, and FFFF, Chairman of the Tribunal.

3. In this dispute, important and complex quantification issues are brought before the Tribunal. The Tribunal considered the usefulness of being assisted by an expert in the field of quantification and announced to the Parties its intention of appointing such an expert. The Claimants welcomed the appointment. The Respondent, while recognising on ... "that the Tribunal has the power to decide on the appointment of an expert whenever it deems necessary to assist in accomplishing its tasks", considered the appointment as premature.

4. Having seen a biographical note showing his qualifications and having seen his disclosure, dated ..., the Parties raised no objection against the appointment of Mr XXXX as Quantification Expert assisting the Arbitral Tribunal. The Tribunal submitted to the Parties a draft of the expert's terms of reference. Both Parties made suggestions concerning this draft which the Tribunal took into account when finalising the present text.

5. The Tribunal now confirms as follows the mission of its Quantification Expert (the Tribunal's Expert or simply the Expert):

   5.1 The Expert shall be at the Tribunal's service in identifying and addressing issues related to quantification.

   5.2 For this purpose, he shall have access to all of the Parties submissions, including documentary and witness evidence and the Parties' expert reports, as directed by the Tribunal.

   5.3 The Tribunal's Expert may meet with the Parties' experts, discuss with them their opinion, seeking any clarification which he deems necessary with respect to their opinion and the underlying assumptions. In addition, if so requested by the Tribunal, he shall determine the relevant points on which the Parties' experts agree and those on which they differ and shall attempt to reduce these points of difference.

   5.4 Where the Tribunal finds this appropriate, the Expert may meet with the Tribunal for reporting and being questioned on the clarification obtained from the Parties' experts. Unless expressly instructed to do so as per below item 5.7, the Expert shall not express an opinion on the soundness or otherwise of the positions taken by the Parties and their experts.

   5.5 The Expert shall regularly report to the Tribunal on the progress of his work, including any progress on any efforts he may be asked to make in reconciling the differences in the positions of Parties' experts. The Parties shall receive copies of these reports and shall be given an opportunity to comment.

   5.6 The Tribunal may assign the Expert to assist the Parties in the process of "thinning" the claims in Batch 4 of the Measurement Claims, as set out in Section 2 of Procedural Order N° 12.

   5.7 The Tribunal may instruct the Expert to prepare a report setting out his independent expert opinion on any issue of quantification. It shall inform the Parties when it gives such instructions and shall afford them an opportunity for commenting on the opinion so expressed by the Expert.

6. For the purposes of all communications with the Parties and their experts, the following contact persons have been identified:

   For the Claimants:

   Mr HHHH

   For the Respondent:

   Mr JJJJ

7. In case of any difficulties arising during the course of his consultation with the Parties' experts, the Expert shall contact the Chairman of the Arbitral Tribunal who shall give further directions to the Expert and, if so required by the circumstances, to the Parties and their experts. If the difficulties persist, the Expert shall prepare a note addressed to the Tribunal, describing the incident and indicating any consequences which it may have on the Tribunal's findings. The Parties will be given an opportunity to comment on such a note and the Tribunal will give the instructions or summons that it may deem required under the circumstances.

8. The costs and expenses of the Expert are subject to the following modalities:

   8.1 The Expert's services will be charged at the rate of xxx per hour and will be invoiced monthly, based on hours worked, including travel time. Related expenses will be invoiced monthly at cost with no mark-up. Since the services are provided for an arbitration in Cairo, no VAT will be charged by the Expert.

   8.2 The Expert will provide to the Chairman of the Tribunal a budget to cover the foreseeable scope of work. At the request of the Centre as directed by the Chairman of the Tribunal, the Parties shall contribute in equal shares to the deposits covering the budgeted work. The Centre will inform the Expert of the amounts of the deposit so available.

   8.3 The Expert will invoice his fees and costs to the Centre for payment by the Centre out of the available deposits. The Centre shall transmit copies of these invoices to the Tribunal and the Parties. Any objections which the Parties may have to an invoice must be notified to the Centre and the Tribunal within 14 days from the date of such transmission. The Tribunal will verify the invoice. Upon approval by the

Tribunal, the Centre will make payment to the Expert. The Parties shall be informed when payments are made to the Expert.

8.4 Invoices are due within 30 days of receipt. A late charge of 1% per month will accrue on amounts not paid within 60 days of the date of receipt of the invoice.

8.5 If a report or appearance before the Arbitral Tribunal is required, the Expert reserves the right to request payment of outstanding fees and expenses prior to submission of such report or appearance. In addition, the Expert may suspend services until payment is received on past due invoices.

8.6 Apart from the payment by the Centre of fees and costs as per item 8.3, the Centre has no liability for the Expert's cost and fees. The Tribunal does not have any liability to the Expert.

8.7 Any changes to the Expert's conditions, in particular any increase in the volume of work requiring fees above the level of the budgeted amount and the deposit, shall be reported by the Expert to the Tribunal which shall, after consultation of the Parties, make the necessary adjustments.

8.8 All payments made by the Parties to the Centre on account of the Expert's services to the Tribunal shall form part of the Costs of the Arbitration to be allocated by a decision of the Arbitral Tribunal.

9. The Expert undertakes to keep strictly confidential his assignment and all documents and information developed or received in the course of it. Unless expressly authorised to do so by the Parties or the Tribunal, the Expert may not reveal any of these documents or this information to third parties. If access to any documents and information relating to this engagement is sought by a third party, the Expert shall promptly notify the Tribunal of such action, tender to it his response to such request and cooperate with the Tribunal concerning his response thereto.

10. The Expert's appointment forms part of the arbitration in Cairo, referred to above in Section 2. This arbitration is governed by the Rules of the Centre and the Egyptian arbitration law.

11. Subject to the limits of the applicable law, the total liability of the Expert for all claims of any kind arising out of this engagement,

whether in contract, tort or otherwise, shall be limited to the total value of his fees.

12. At the end of his assignment, the Expert is authorised, subject to prior notification to the Centre, to discard and destroy all documents related to his assignment, except if the Centre, within 30 days as from the Expert's notification, requests that these documents be returned to the Centre. The Expert may retain a copy of his reports or work papers for his records.

Cairo, ... 2008

The Expert	for the Tribunal
....	....
Mr XXXX	FFFF
	Chairman of the Arbitral Tribunal